AMAZING

(MOSTLY) EDIBLE SCIENCE

A Family Guide to
Fun Experiments in the Kitchen

ANDREW SCHLOSS

PHOTOGRAPHS BY CHRIS ROCHELLE

QUARRY

Quarto is the authority on a wide range of topics.

Quarto educates, entertains and enriches the lives of our readers—enthusiasts and lovers of hands-on living.

www.QuartoKnows.com

First published in the United States of America in 2016 by
Quarry Books, an imprint of
Quarto Publishing Group USA Inc.
100 Cummings Center
Suite 406-L
Beverly, Massachusetts 01915-6101
Telephone: (978) 282-9590
Fax: (978) 283-2742
QuartoKnows.com
Visit our blogs at QuartoKnows.com

10 9 8 7 6 5 4 3 2 1

Library of Congress Cataloging-in-Publication Data:
Schloss, Andrew, 1951–
Amazing (mostly) edible science : a family guide to fun experiments in the kitchen / by Andrew Schloss.
pages cm
ISBN 978-1-63159-109-9 (paperback)—ISBN 978-1-62788-845-5 (eISBN)
1. Food—Experiments. 2. Science—Experiments. 3. Scientific re-creations. I. Title.
TX551.S34 2016
641.3—dc23
2015027557

Design: Allison Stern
Food Styling: Amy Wisniewski and Chris Rochelle
Printed in China

In Memory of Meme's Custard

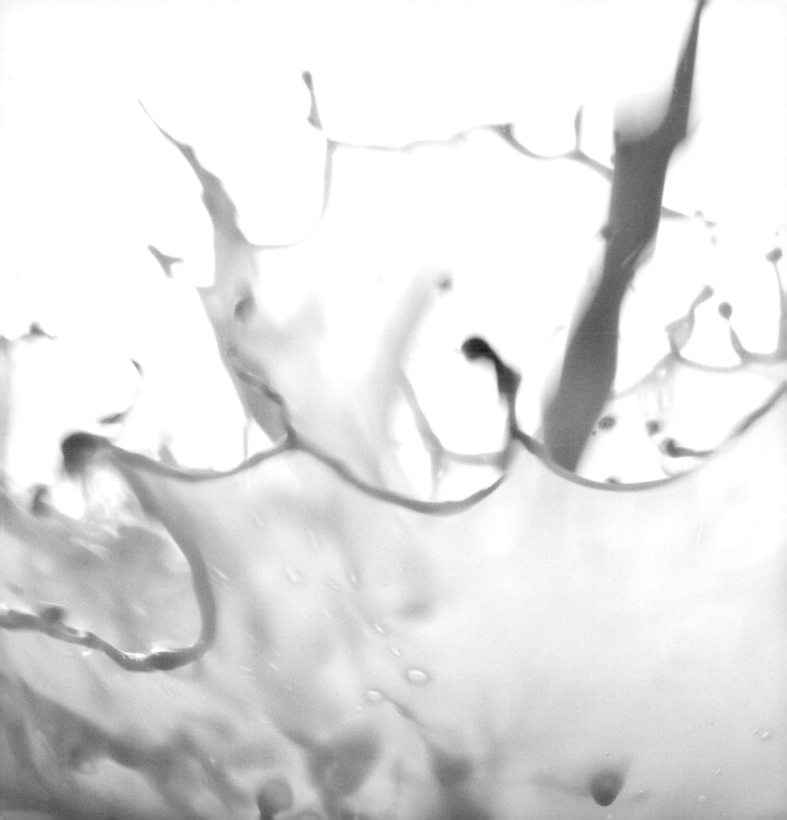

CONTENTS

INTRODUCTION

When I was ten years old, I watched my grandmother make baked custard. I saw her put a bowl of watery milk and eggs into the oven and, an hour later, pull out a bowl of pudding so solid you could slice it with a knife. I was floored! I knew I was seeing magic, and that sense of wonder has never left me.

Since then, I have learned that what I was actually seeing was science, and observing scientific principles in action every time I work in the kitchen is still a thrill. That's what cooking, and science, and this book are all about.

MAKING SCIENCE EDIBLE

I have been a professional chef for more than thirty years, and written many cookbooks, but this one holds a special place in my heart. Each experiment is written directly to kids. Almost all can be completed with simple household ingredients. Most take less than an hour (some can be done in as little as 10 minutes), and each provides a snack or meal after you're finished experimenting.

You don't need to know science to make great-tasting food, but there's certainly a lot of science you can learn while you're doing it: Scrambled eggs are about protein coagulation. Roasting chicken is an illustration of the Maillard reaction (the science behind browning). Grilling is all about thermal dynamics, and baking cookies is a series of lessons on acid/base interactions, the behavior of fats, the hygroscopic nature of sugars, and the gelatinization of starches.

Humans are innately curious, especially young humans, and learning is intrinsically exciting and fun. Cooking with your kids (or your parents) is not just a way to feed them and give them practical life skills; it's also a delicious and fun way to bring science to life.

HOW TO USE THIS BOOK

If you have a basic kitchen, you probably have most of the tools you need to do the experiments in this book. If an activity requires anything more complicated than a saucepan, mixing spoon, or measuring cup, I warn you up front. And if I do ask you to get something a little weird, like agar powder (vegetarian gelatin) or sodium alginate, I've given you a source, and guarantee that the WOW! factor in that experiment is worth going after the odd ingredient.

As you look through this book, you'll see that each experiment is ranked in seven key areas:

AMAZING: Cool / Crazy! / Yowza! / WOW!

EDIBLE: Yuk! / Give It a Taste / Eat Up! / YUM!

EXPERIMENT: Easy-Peasy / Plan in Advance / A Little Help, Please!

TIME: Less than 30 Minutes / 30–60 Minutes / Afternoon Project / Two Phases

MATERIALS: Gather at Home / Go Shop / Order in Advance

COST: Less than $5 / Less than $10 / Less than $20

SAFETY: Safe / Some Cooking / Be Careful / Watch Out!

HOW COOL IS IT?

No matter where an experiment is ranked on the Amazing scale, they're all worth a try. "Cool" means you're making something surprising—something you might never have thought of. "Crazy!" or "Yowza!" means you're going to be amazed at what you did. A "WOW!" should blow everyone's mind.

HOW EDIBLE IS IT?

At the "YUM!" end of the Edible scale, the result of your experiment is guaranteed to be delicious. The closer you get to "Yuk!" the less appetizing an experiment may be. Saying something is edible doesn't always mean you'd want to eat it.

HOW COMPLICATED IS IT?

The Experiment ranking measures how easy the activity is: "Easy-Peasy" means most children six years of age or older will need minimal adult supervision. "Plan in Advance" means most kids can do it with an adult standing by. "A Little Help, Please!" means that heat or something potentially dangerous is involved. If there are places where adult involvement is advised, I've noted it in ALL CAPS. In some cases, I've added a warning line with a 🖐 icon to help safeguard curious explorers.

HOW LONG WILL IT TAKE?

The Time guideline measures how long the experiment will take once the materials are gathered. For experiments marked "Afternoon Project" or "Two Phases," most of the time required is wait time—to allow a gel to set or a crystal to grow, for example—and does not require your active participation or even your presence.

WHAT WILL YOU NEED?

Materials range from ingredients and equipment you probably have on hand to those you may need to shop for, either locally or (planning ahead) by ordering online.

> **NOTE:** *You're definitely going to need some sort of high-temperature thermometer to do many of the experiments in this book. Either an instant-read digital thermometer or a candy thermometer will work, as long as you can measure temperatures over 300°F (150°C). They're inexpensive and handy to have around, whether you're cooking dinner or doing experiments. You can find them online or in your local kitchenware store.*

HOW MUCH WILL IT COST?

The Cost scale only applies to special materials required. It doesn't include ingredients like oil, sugar, or salt that you're likely to have on hand, or equipment such as the pots, pans, and stirring spoons you normally use in your kitchen. When there's a specialty need, I break it out and tell you about it separately.

HOW SAFE IS IT?

Safety rankings mostly depend on the skill level and responsibility of your children. If you let your kids use the stove, everything in the book is probably fair game. In places where I think adult involvement is helpful, that's noted. But my rankings are just guidelines. It's your kid. It's your house. You have to be the judge.

> **NOTE:** *Several experiments use food coloring and natural ingredients, such as grape juice, that can tint skin and cloth. Using play clothes, aprons, and table coverings will help avoid unwanted stains. The color will usually wash off hands with soap and hot water, but if that doesn't work, try a little mild cleanser, like Soft Scrub.*

CHAPTER 1

WIGGLY, JIGGLY EXPERIMENTS

Have you ever wondered what makes gelatin wiggle, how a gummy worm stretches, or why a marshmallow pops back after you bite it? And what in the world makes slime so…well…slimy? All these wiggly, slimy, bouncy, stretchy textures come from one thing—the ability of certain substances to gel.

Gels are liquids that don't flow freely. In a gel, the liquid is contained in a network of stretchy molecules. When you move a gel, the liquid in the network starts to flow, but the molecules will only stretch so far. When they reach their limit, they snap back into shape, pushing the liquid in the opposite direction. That back-and-forth push and pull is what all that wiggling, bouncing, and stretching is about.

Gels are actually easy to make. All it takes is some water or juice and some gelling powder. In the following experiments, you get to play around with a lot of them—agar, psyllium, starch—and something that's not a gel at all, but still moves like crazy: *katsuobushi*. Fun to say, and way more fun to watch!

IN THIS CHAPTER:

JUICY GEL BEADS

These little pearls of juice are the coolest, most mind-blowing fun you could possibly have with a bowl of warm gel and a tall glass of cold oil. The gel is made from agar (also called agar-agar), a gelling powder that comes from algae. Agar is used in many Asian desserts and as a vegetarian substitute for gelatin (which is made from animal collagen). It's also a popular culturing medium in science labs. That's why the best places to find agar are in Asian grocery stores, science supply stores, and on the vegan shelves of your local natural-foods store. It's also available from many Internet sites.

Makes about 2 cups (480 ml)

 BE CAREFUL! HAVE A GROWN-UP HELP YOU DO THIS.

WOW!

EAT UP!

A LITTLE HELP, PLEASE!

30–60 MINUTES

GO SHOP

LESS THAN $10

SOME COOKING

GET THIS:

1 to 2 cups (240 ml to 480 ml) vegetable oil

1 cup (240 ml) colorful, pulp-free fruit juice or sports drink, such as cranberry juice, orange juice (without pulp), or blue and/or yellow sports drink

½ teaspoon (1¾ g) agar

Tall drinking glass

Small saucepan

Small whisk or fork

Small heatproof bowl

Medicine dropper, disposable kitchen pipette, or small spoon

Medium bowl

Slotted spoon

Fine mesh strainer

Container with a tight-fitting lid to store your beads

DO THIS:

GET THE OIL REALLY COLD

1. Fill the tall drinking glass at least three-fourths full with the oil.
2. Put it in the freezer until really cold, 30 to 40 minutes.

MAKE THE GELATIN

1. When the oil has been in the freezer for at least 10 minutes, put the juice in the saucepan. Stir in the agar with the small whisk or fork until mostly dissolved. (If there are a few lumps, don't worry; they'll go away as the mixture heats.)
2. Put the juice mixture over medium-high heat and heat to boiling, stirring gently all the time. As soon as the mixture boils, pour into the heatproof bowl.
3. Wait for about 20 minutes for the mixture to cool until it feels slightly hot to the touch, like medium-hot tap water, about 125°F (52°C).

MAKE THE BEADS

1. Take the glass of oil out of the freezer. If it has been in there for more than 45 minutes, it may be cloudy and thick. Let it sit out at room temperature until the cloudiness clears. (If the oil is

(continued)

too cold when you start, the beads will form, but may float on top and flatten out, rather than being perfectly round.)

2. Fill the medicine dropper with the juice mixture, hold it about an inch (2.5 cm) above the surface of the oil, and squirt a small amount into the cold oil. As soon as the juice mix hits the oil it will form a perfect little ball that will sink down to the bottom of the glass. (You can also drop the juice mix into the oil with a small spoon, but it's a little harder to control that way.)

3. Continue until you have about 20 beads. You can make more after you remove them, but don't crowd the glass or the beads at the bottom will get smashed.

RINSE AND ENJOY!

1. Fill the medium bowl with clean, cold water. Using the slotted spoon, carefully transfer your beads to the bowl of water to rinse them.

2. Drain the beads gently in the fine-mesh strainer. Pop the beads in your mouth and they'll burst, releasing a gush of juice. They're also delicious sprinkled over ice cream.

3. You can store the finished beads in a tightly sealed container in the refrigerator for up to a few hours.

HOW DID THAT HAPPEN? *Agar is a natural gelling agent, like gelatin. When heated, both agar and gelatin dissolve in water, trapping the liquid in a web of linking molecules as they cool. As the web forms, the water has less and less space to move around, causing the liquid to set into a semi solid.*

Gelatin and agar both work in pretty much the same way. But unlike gelatin, agar can form a gel at really low concentrations. Half a teaspoon of agar can thicken a cup of liquid. You would need three times that amount of gelatin to do the same thing. Also, agar stays solid up to 110°F (43°C), which means it will keep its shape in your mouth. If you've ever had your temperature taken, you know that the inside of your mouth is between 98° and 99°F (36.6° and 37.2°C). That's hot enough to melt gelatin, but not agar.

Although the formation of these gelled beads may look like magic, it's science! First, the agar is dissolved in juice. When the juice mixture is dripped into the cold oil, it gels on contact. Because oil and juice don't mix, the drops cling to themselves rather than dispersing, forming perfect spheres.

GLOW-IN-THE-DARK GELATIN

A regular box of fruit-flavored gelatin (like Jell-O), some tonic water, and a black light are all you need to make this glowing treat. You can also make your own fruit-flavored gelatin by mixing unflavored gelatin powder with sugar or honey and using fruit juice for your liquid. This allows you to add some nutrition to your gel and gives you the freedom to mix up some unique flavor combos—blueberry-cinnamon, honey-apple, apricot-ginger. (Now you're a chef and a scientist.) You can buy black lights (also called ultraviolet lights, or UV-A lights) at the hardware store or online.

YOWZA!

GIVE IT A TASTE

EASY-PEASY

AFTERNOON PROJECT

GO SHOP

LESS THAN $5

SOME COOKING

A 3-ounce (85-g) box of fruit-flavored gelatin makes 2 cups (480 ml)
A 6-ounce (170-g) box makes 1 qt (1 L)

GET THIS:

- 1 box lemon- or lime-flavored gelatin (or you can use unflavored gelatin with sugar and flavorings; see recipe introduction and Step 1 in the "Make the Gelatin" instructions)
- 1 bottle tonic water (both sugar-free and regular will work, but seltzer will not, so don't even bother trying)

The bowls and spoons and other stuff you always use to make gelatin desserts
A black light
Some cookie cutters (optional)

DO THIS:

MAKE THE GELATIN

1. Follow the directions on the box, but use the tonic water instead of regular water. (If you're using plain, unflavored gelatin, add 3 tablespoons of sugar and 1 teaspoon of lemon or lime juice for every ¼-ounce/7-g packet of gelatin.)
2. When you've got everything all mixed together, pour the liquid gelatin into a bowl and put it into the refrigerator to cool and get firm.

MAKE IT GLOW!

1. When your gelatin is cooled and set, shine your black light on it—and watch it glow.
2. If you want to go all out, find some cool cookie cutters and cut your gelatin into glowing bells, stars, bugs, or whatever other shapes you want. Serve dessert in the dark and treat your family to a show!

(continued)

HOW DID THAT HAPPEN? *Try a bite of your glowy gelatin, or take a sip of the leftover tonic water, and you'll notice that it tastes kind of bitter. That's because tonic water has a bitter-tasting chemical in it called quinine, and quinine glows greenish-blue when it's under an ultraviolet (black) light.*

If you don't believe it's the tonic water making your dessert glow, make another box of yellow or green fruit gelatin with regular water and see what it looks like when you shine the black light on it. It won't taste funny when you eat it, but you'll probably need to leave the dining-room lights on.

what is ultraviolet light?

When you turn on your black light in a dark room you'll see that it makes a purplish glow. What you can't see is the ultraviolet light that the black-light bulb is also producing.

Visible light—the kind of energy we can see—is one part of a big range of waves that move energy from one place to another. (You've heard about "traveling at the speed of light," haven't you?)

Light energy travels in waves from its source to our eyes. But our eyes can only see the energy waves that are moving at a certain speed, about a billion feet per second. If they're traveling slower or faster than that, their energy is invisible. The energy waves are still there. We just can't see them.

All colors of light travel at the same speed (the speed of light), but as waves of slightly different sizes and shapes. Light waves that are long and low we see as reds and oranges. Light waves that are short and spiky we see as blues and purples. Together, they make up all the colors of the rainbow.

When energy is traveling more slowly than the speed of visible light, it's called infrared (below red) energy. When it's traveling faster than the light we can see, it's called ultraviolet (above violet). Your black light is emitting ultraviolet energy. You can't see it, but it's there—and the quinine in the tonic water proves it's there.

why does quinine glow?

Quinine contains phosphors, substances that emit visible light in response to energy that we can't see. The phosphors in the quinine are taking in that UV (ultraviolet) energy and converting it into visible light by lengthening its wavelength to the size of green-blue visible light.

If you happen to be wearing white while doing this experiment, you'll see that the black light is making your white clothes glow in the dark, too. That's because modern detergents contain phosphors that convert UV energy into visible white light. Without phosphors, your T-shirt may look white, but the phosphors allow you to see both the visible light in sunlight and the UV rays, making the shirt look "whiter than white."

MAKE-YOUR-OWN MARSHMALLOWS

The puffy, powdery, sweeter-than-sweet candy pillows known as marshmallows are filled with scientific fun. When you make them at home, you're experimenting with all kinds of cool natural principles: You're showing how collagen behaves (that's the protein that makes up all the connective tissue in your body); you're discovering how sugar forms crystals (and what happens when it gets hot enough to melt); you're demonstrating how foams are made; and you're discovering how gelatin gels work. These marshmallows are going to make you so-o-o-o-o smart!

Makes 81 marshmallows

 BE CAREFUL! HAVE A GROWN-UP HELP YOU DO THIS.

GET THIS:

Three ¼-ounce (7-g) packets unflavored gelatin
   (7½ teaspoons)

1 cup (240 ml) cold water

1 cup (240 ml) light corn syrup

1½ cups (300 g) granulated sugar

¼ teaspoon salt

2 teaspoons (10 ml) vanilla extract

6 drops of food coloring (optional)

Nonstick cooking spray

⅓ cup (35 g) powdered sugar

3 tablespoons (25 g) cornstarch

Standing mixer with whisk attachment

Large, heavy saucepan

Mixing spoon

Candy thermometer or high-temp
   instant-read thermometer

9 inch (23 cm) square baking pan

Small mixing bowl

Flat metal spatula

Large cutting board

Large knife

Gallon-sized zipper-lock plastic bag or a
   container with a lid for storing your
   leftover marshmallows

(continued)

YOWZA!

YUM!

A LITTLE HELP, PLEASE!

AFTERNOON PROJECT

GO SHOP

LESS THAN $10

SOME COOKING

DO THIS:

MAKE THE MARSHMALLOW MIXTURE

1. Combine the gelatin and ½ cup (120 ml) of the cold water in the bowl of the standing mixer. Attach the whisk attachment and mix briefly to combine.
2. Mix the remaining ½ cup cold water, the corn syrup, granulated sugar, and salt in the large, heavy saucepan. Put over medium-high heat, stir to dissolve the ingredients, cover, and cook for 3 minutes.
3. Uncover and heat until the syrup is 240°F (115°C) on a candy or instant-read thermometer. Start measuring after about 5 minutes of cooking.
4. Immediately remove from the heat. It's important that the syrup be right at 240°F (115°C). If it's too cold, the marshmallows won't set. If it gets too hot, the marshmallows will be crunchy instead of chewy.
5. Turn the mixer on low speed and, while the machine is running, pour the syrup slowly down the side of the bowl into the gelatin mixture.
6. Once all of the syrup has been added, slowly turn up the speed of the mixer to high. Continue to beat until the mixture is thick and white and barely warm, about 10 minutes. In the last minute, add the vanilla (and food coloring, if you want).

COOL THE MARSHMALLOWS

1. Spray the baking pan with nonstick cooking spray. Not too much.
2. Combine the powdered sugar and cornstarch in a small bowl. Sprinkle half into the baking pan and tilt the pan to evenly coat the bottom.
3. Spray the spatula with nonstick spray and scrape the marshmallow mixture into the prepared pan. Spread the top evenly, making sure the marshmallow gets all the way into the corners of the pan. If the spatula starts sticking to the marshmallow, spray with more oil.
4. Dust the top with the rest of the powdered sugar mixture. Set aside to dry for at least 6 hours or, even better, overnight.

CUT THE MARSHMALLOWS

1. Turn the marshmallow sheet out onto the big cutting board and cut into 1-inch (2.5-cm) squares, coating the knife with more powdered sugar to keep it from sticking, and dusting the cut surfaces of the marshmallows with the powdered sugar mixture that falls out of the pan onto the cutting board.
2. Eat, and store any leftovers in a tightly sealed plastic bag or container at room temperature for up to 3 months.

(continued)

HOW DID THAT HAPPEN? *Gelatin is powdered collagen, the main protein in the connective tissue that holds animals' cells together (including yours). Like all liquid proteins, such as egg white or cream, gelatin thickens, or coagulates, when beaten or whipped.*

When you make marshmallows, concentrated hot-sugar syrup is beaten into the gelatin with a mixer equipped with a wire whisk. As the mixer spins, the wires of the whisk force air into the mixture. At the same time, the strings of protein molecules in the collagen get tangled up around pockets of air.

As more and more air gets incorporated into the protein tangle, the mixture starts to inflate, getting bigger and bigger. Soon, the little bit of gelatin in the bottom of the mixing bowl is filling the whole bowl! The beating continues as the gelatin cools, until eventually it solidifies, trapping the air inside the bubble walls. The finished marshmallows are both chewy (from coagulated protein) and fluffy (from lots of air bubbles).

corn syrup insurance

When you make marshmallows, you cook down the syrup until it's about 85 percent sugar. At that concentration, sugar molecules (mostly sucrose) are likely to form crystals (see Chapter 2), which would make the finished marshmallows coarse and crunchy. But who wants crunchy marshmallows?

Adding corn syrup keeps that crystallization from happening by loading up the sucrose syrup with other types of sugar (mostly glucose). Long chains of sugar molecules get in the way, tangling themselves around the sucrose molecules and keeping them from forming crystals. The results are smooth, chewy, puffy, fluffy marshmallows, every time.

INFLATABLE MARSHMALLOWS

WOW!

EAT UP!

A LITTLE HELP, PLEASE!

AFTERNOON PROJECT

GO SHOP

LESS THAN $10

BE CAREFUL

So you just made marshmallows—now it's time to get down to the real work, and start to play. It may seem like air is a big, empty void, but really it's filled with gases that are moving around all of the time. When you trap air (like you did in the marshmallows), you can begin to control that movement, which is exactly what this experiment is all about. You can inflate the air in your marshmallows two ways. The coolest is to use a vacuum sealer (like a FoodSaver) with a jar-sealer attachment. This process allows you to inflate and deflate the marshmallows more than once. You can also use a microwave for an easier inflation, but the microwave cooks the marshmallow, so once it deflates it won't blow up a second time.

 BE CAREFUL! HAVE A GROWN-UP HELP YOU DO THIS.

GET THIS:

Some full-sized marshmallows (not minis!), store-bought or homemade (page 21)

Vacuum sealer with jar-sealer attachment and Mason jar, or microwave oven and paper plate

DO THIS:

TO INFLATE MARSHMALLOWS USING A VACUUM SEALER

1. Put a marshmallow in a Mason jar or other jar that works with your vacuum sealer (see the manufacturer's instructions for your machine).
2. Put the jar-sealer attachment on your vacuum sealer, and fit the jar-sealer to the mouth of your Mason jar. Turn on the vacuum sealer and watch the marshmallow swell to 10 or more times its original size!
3. When you turn off the vacuum the marshmallow will return to its original size and shape. Try it again, with two or more marshmallows.

TO INFLATE MARSHMALLOWS USING A MICROWAVE

1. Put 1 or more marshmallows on a paper plate.
2. Place in the microwave and cook at full power for 30 seconds to 1 minute (depending on the number of marshmallows on the plate). Watch them inflate into blobs about 5 times their original size.
3. The puffed-up candies will have the soft consistency of marshmallows that have been toasted on a stick. Tear one open and you'll see that the interior is brown and crispy—like a toasted marshmallow turned inside out.

HOW DID THAT HAPPEN? *Remember, a marshmallow is filled with air bubbles. When you put one in a sealed jar, there are two air-filled environments under the lid: the one inside the marshmallow, and the one outside the marshmallow, but still inside the jar.*

Before you turn on the vacuum sealer, the air bubbles inside the marshmallow are at the same atmospheric pressure as the air in the jar. When you turn on the vacuum sealer, the air pressure inside the jar drops dramatically, making the air pressure inside the marshmallow rise accordingly. Air bubbles push outward, causing the stretchy walls of the marshmallow to expand. When you turn off the vacuum and let air back into the jar, the surrounding air pressure increases again, and the marshmallow deflates, going back to its previous size.

In the microwave, the air bubbles inside the marshmallow also expand, but for a different reason. The microwave heats the water in the marshmallow, turning it into steam. Steam is the gaseous state of liquid water, and because gas takes up more space than the same amount of liquid, the steam makes the stretchy air-bubble walls inside the marshmallows expand, making them inflate. The steam trapped in the center of the marshmallows gets so hot that it can make the sugar in the mixture caramelize, turning the interior brown and crispy.

INCREDIBLE, EDIBLE SLIME

Thick, slippery, and gooey, slime is a strange substance that feels funny to the touch. The secret ingredient is cornstarch! The simple mixture of cornstarch and water is one of the weirdest fluids on Earth. In fact, it behaves so strangely that it is classified as "non-Newtonian," an homage to Isaac Newton, who first described the easy flow of fluids, when he wasn't identifying gravity or developing calculus. A liquid of cornstarch and water doesn't act like other liquids; the harder you press on it, the more solid it becomes. Wild! This project is fast and fun, and great to pull out at parties!

Makes about 1½ cups (360 ml)

 BE CAREFUL! HAVE A GROWN-UP HELP YOU DO THIS.

YOWZA!

GIVE IT A TASTE

A LITTLE HELP, PLEASE!

LESS THAN 30 MINUTES

GATHER AT HOME

LESS THAN $5

SOME COOKING

GET THIS:

One 14-ounce (414 ml) can sweetened
condensed milk
1 tablespoon (8 g) cornstarch
Some food coloring
A few drops of vanilla or other flavor extract
(optional)

Saucepan
Mixing spoon
Fork

DO THIS:

COOK UP YOUR SLIME

1. In the saucepan, stir together the milk and cornstarch over low heat. Cook, stirring constantly.
2. When the mixture thickens, take it off the stove. BE CAREFUL! HOT SLIME CAN STICK AND BURN.

COOL IT, COLOR IT—AND PLAY WITH IT!

1. Stir in your favorite slime-ball coloring and any flavorings you might want with a fork, and then let it cool.
2. When your slime ball is at room temperature, you can take it out—and play with it! And yes—it's edible.

(continued)

HOW DID THAT HAPPEN? *Most materials have three states of being: solid, liquid, and gas. At room temperature, for instance, water is a liquid. Freeze it, and it becomes a solid (ice). Heat it up, and it evaporates into a gas (steam). Milk, which has a lot of water in it, acts in pretty much the same way—or it would if you hadn't mixed the cornstarch in it.*

The weird thing about cornstarch is that it does not fully dissolve in most liquids. Instead, its tiny particles just sort of stay floating around inside, creating what's called a suspension. When you squeeze on your slime ball, the bits of cornstarch smash together, making it feel slippery on the outside but solid on the inside. Let go, and the cornstarch bits spread out again, making your slime ball seem more liquid than solid.

PS: *If you're planning to eat your slime ball, you might not want to roll it on the floor, let it goop through your dirty hands, or get a bunch of hair in it. In the end, you may find it's a better toy than a snack—but be brave, and give it a try.*

IT'S ALIVE! PIZZA

All you need for this amazing (and slightly creepy) pizza is a fresh or frozen pizza and a sprinkling of *katsuobushi*, or dried bonito tuna flakes (available online and in Asian markets, usually in the soup aisle). Even though they are shaved from real fish, *katsuobushi* don't look or taste anything like fish. They look more like thin woodchips, and taste almost like nothing. But when you put them on pizza, or anything hot and moist (rice, pasta, soup, or scrambled eggs), they spring to life and start to dance!

Makes 8 servings

 BE CAREFUL! HAVE A GROWN-UP HELP YOU DO THIS.

WOW!

CRAZY!

A LITTLE HELP, PLEASE!

LESS THAN 30 MINUTES

GO SHOP

LESS THAN $10

SOME COOKING

GET THIS:

1 large fresh or frozen pizza

1 cup (230 g) *katsuobushi* (see recipe introduction)

Oven mitts

DO THIS:

BAKE THE PIZZA

1. If using a frozen pizza, bake according to the package directions. If you've got a take-out pizza, stick it in a 350°F (180°C) oven for 5 minutes to make sure it's really hot. If you made your own pizza, bake according to your regular recipe.

IT'S ALIVE!

1. As soon as the pizza comes out of the oven, scatter the shaved bonito all over the top. The flakes will start to wiggle around.
2. Cut into wedges and serve while they're active!

HOW DID THAT HAPPEN? *Osmosis is the tendency of fluids, particularly water, to pass from an area of greater concentration to one of lesser concentration. That's what's happening on your pizza.*

Bonito is a kind of tuna. The dried, shaved bonito flakes known as katsuobushi *are made by drying a tuna fillet for several weeks until it has lost almost all of its water and looks like a shriveled-up piece of wood. After it's dried, the tuna meat is shaved into tissue-thin flakes that can be sprinkled on food. When you put them on your pizza, the flakes absorb moisture from the hot, steamy pizza. As the dry flakes swell with water, they start to dance around.*

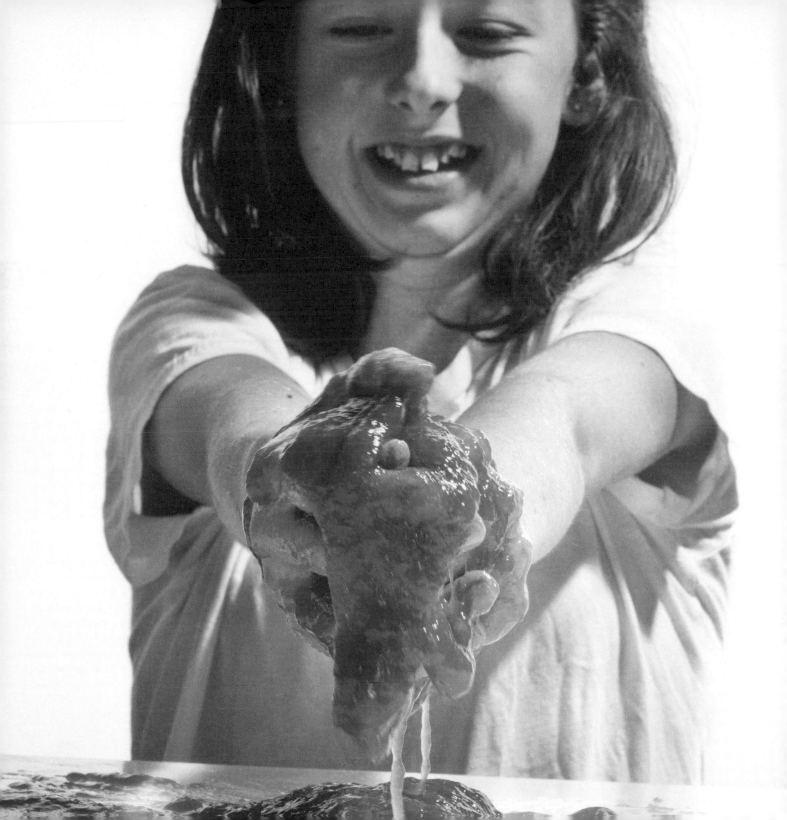

EATUM-UP ECTOPLASM

There are several ways to make ooey-gooey, gross-out, slimy slime. Some versions are not safe to eat. This one, though, while a little less slimy, is completely safe. You can even eat it. The thing that makes it slimy is psyllium (say "silly-um"), a type of plant fiber that absorbs liquid like a sponge. It starts out dry, but when its thirst is quenched, it gets so slippery and wet that it's impossible to hold onto. The texture is pretty gross, but lime juice and honey make it sort of tasty.

YOWZA!

GIVE IT A TASTE

EASY-PEASY

LESS THAN 30 MINUTES

GO SHOP

LESS THAN $5

SOME COOKING

Makes about 1 cup (240 ml)

GET THIS:

1 tablespoon (12 g) psyllium fiber powder, like Metamucil, available at grocery stores and pharmacies
2 cups (480 ml) water
2 teaspoons honey
1 teaspoon lime juice
Green food coloring

Small whisk or fork
Medium microwave-safe bowl or glass measuring cup
Plastic wrap
Microwave oven
Small plastic container with a tight-fitting lid (to store the ectoplasm when you're done playing)

DO THIS:

COOK YOUR ECTOPLASM

1. With the small whisk or fork, mix the psyllium and water in the microwave-safe bowl or glass measuring cup.
2. Cover loosely with plastic wrap or other microwave-safe cover and microwave at full power for 3 minutes. It should be bubbling.
3. Remove the cover (BE CARFFUL NOT TO BURN YOURSELF ON THE ESCAPING STEAM!) and stir. Cover again and microwave for another 3 minutes.

COLOR AND FLAVOR

1. Remove cover and stir in the honey, lime juice, and a few drops of food coloring. Let cool to room temperature.

PLAY!

1. Pour slime through your fingers and on unsuspecting victims.
2. Drip into your mouth to freak out your friends and your parents.

(continued)

HOW DID THAT HAPPEN? *Plants have two fibrous materials that give them structure. Cellulose is tough and hard, and makes plant cells rigid and strong. Hemicellulose is bendy, allowing plant cells to move without breaking. When plant fibers are cooked in water, the cellulose stays firm and doesn't dissolve, but the hemicellulose opens up, taking in tons of water and making the cooked vegetable creamy and soft. In the case of psyllium—which is the outside husk of a seed that can absorb many times its weight in water—lots of hemicellulose gives the cooked powder a gelatinous consistency that is the very essence of SLIME!*

PS: *Heads Up! If you play with the ectoplasm for a long time, it will turn your hands sort of yellow-green. Lots of hot, soapy water will eventually wash it off, but if that doesn't work, a little mild cleanser, like Soft Scrub, will do the job.*

flubber

You can solidify your slime into rubbery, bouncy, flubber by nuking it more. Return the slime to its bowl and microwave for 3 minutes, stir, and microwave again. The more you nuke it, the firmer and bouncier your flubber will become.

LICK YOUR FINGER PAINT

Look at those colors! Cherry-Berry Red. Midnight-Summer-Sky Blue. Don't-Look-into-the-Sun Yellow. Dare-You-to-Roll-Down-that-Wet-Grassy-Hill Green. But whatever you do, don't lick those paint-coated fingers! Wait a minute...go for it! This paint is delicious! Or at least it's edible. The base cooks up in a few minutes, and you can store it in tightly closed jars for weeks.

Makes 4 jars of paint, about ⅔ cup (160 ml) each

 BE CAREFUL! HAVE A GROWN-UP HELP YOU DO THIS.

COOL

GIVE IT A TASTE

A LITTLE HELP, PLEASE

LESS THAN 30 MINUTES

GATHER AT HOME

LESS THAN $5

SOME COOKING

GET THIS:

2½ cups (600 ml) cold water

¼ cup (55 g) cornstarch

¼ cup (50 g) sugar

4 different colors of food coloring

Flavorings: Lemon extract for yellow, berry extract for red, mint extract for green, grape extract for blue, etc. (optional)

Blender

Medium saucepan

Mixing spoons

4 plastic drinking cups (and/or plastic containers with lids for storage)

DO THIS:

BLEND

1. Put the water, cornstarch, and sugar in the blender. Blend until smooth.

COOK

1. Pour the mixture into the saucepan and cook over medium heat until it boils and thickens, stirring the whole time. Remove from the heat and let your base cool.

MAKE PAINT

1. Divide the base among the 4 cups.
2. Stir 6 drops of food coloring into each cup, mixing as you like, but creating four distinct colors. Add a drop or two of flavoring to each color, if you want, and your paint is ready to go!

CREATE YOUR MASTERPIECE

1. Paint away! Feel free to lick your fingers as you work.
2. When you're done, be sure to keep the containers covered to keep your paint from drying out.

(continued)

HOW DID THAT HAPPEN? *Mix some cornstarch into cold water and nothing much happens. But heat up the water and the starch molecules start moving around. At a certain point, usually just before boiling, the organization of starch molecules starts to break apart. Instead of sticking to one another, the starch starts to bond with the water. Within a couple of seconds, the thin, watery liquid in the pot turns thick and creamy, like pudding. And if you added some chocolate and sugar, that's exactly what it would be. But if you add color, it becomes paint; scrumptious, edible paint!*

CHAPTER 2
SWEET CRYSTAL EXPERIMENTS

Crystals are beautiful. Jagged and shimmering, they can catch even the smallest amount of light and sparkle through the darkness. Diamonds are crystals, as are all precious gems—but so is ice, and granite, and hard candy.

Although crystals are common in nature, they are not so common in food. In fact, there are only two foods that come in the form of natural crystals: sugar and salt (plus ice, but that doesn't really count as food).

Crystals are hard. When you're making hard candy, you want to encourage crystallization to give each bite a good C-R-U-N-C-H! That's the case when you make Amber Maple-Syrup Crystals (page 43) or Rock Candy (page 45). In other foods, like ice cream, crunchiness feels weird. In those experiments, we try out ways to control crystal growth so the finished food is thickened by crystals, but remains smooth and creamy. In still other experiments, like Sweet Lava (page 55) and Popping Pebbles (page 59), you're going to trap air in the crystals, which makes the rocky structure of the candy puff up and gives you a wild texture that's both crunchy and foamy.

IN THIS CHAPTER:

AMBER MAPLE-SYRUP CRYSTALS

These crystals aren't jagged and sharp like Rock Candy (page 45), but perfectly clear and super smooth, like hardened pieces of amber—which is, in fact, close to what they are. Amber, the precious rock that takes millions of years to form, is made from petrified drips of prehistoric tree sap. Maple syrup, the sweet, sticky stuff you pour on your pancakes in the morning, is also made from tree sap (though slightly less prehistoric). When you boil maple syrup, the sugar molecules get packed closely together—so close that they begin to bump into each other and stick together into a golden, edible pane.

Makes about ½ cup (120 g)

 BE CAREFUL! HAVE A GROWN-UP HELP YOU DO THIS.

YOWZA!

YUM!

A LITTLE HELP, PLEASE!

LESS THAN 30 MINUTES

GATHER AT HOME

LESS THAN $5

WATCH OUT!

GET THIS:

1 cup (240 ml) pure maple syrup (not imitation maple syrup!)
Chopped nuts or raisins (optional)

Metal pie pan or baking pan
Small saucepan
Long handled mixing spoon

DO THIS:

1. Put the pie pan in the freezer to get cold, 15 minutes to a few hours.
2. Heat the maple syrup in the saucepan over medium heat, stirring most of the time, until the syrup starts to thicken and becomes whitish and foamy, about 10 minutes.
3. Dribble the hot syrup on the cold pan and watch the pieces of maple amber form! (If you want, you can sprinkle in some chopped nuts or raisins and pretend they're bugs stuck in amber.)

 HOW DID THAT HAPPEN? *Maple syrup is the boiled-down sap of maple trees. Sap is the way a tree transports its food from its roots to its leaves. During spring and summer, maple leaves collect energy from sunlight and convert it into sugar by a process called photosynthesis. The sugar is used to nourish the tree as it grows; any extra is stored as starch in its roots. In spring, when the tree needs a boost of energy, it converts some of that stored starch back into sugar and sends it in the form of sap (a combination of water, sugar, and minerals) up the trunk and into the branches, where new leaves are forming. Syrup makers tap holes through the tree bark to release the sap, which they collect and boil, causing the sap to thicken into syrup.*

ROCK CANDY

Ever see a rock grow? Maybe if you were a couple of billion years old, you might have. But since you're probably younger than that, here's your chance. Rocks are made of crystals—atoms or molecules that line up in repeating patterns to make geometric shapes. The lead in a pencil is a very soft crystal; the diamond in an engagement ring is a very hard crystal. In this "sweet" project, you'll watch as a string of beautiful sugar crystals turn into rocks before your eyes.

YOWZA!

YUM!

A LITTLE HELP, PLEASE!

TWO PHASES

GATHER AT HOME

LESS THAN $5

WATCH OUT!

Makes about 2 cups (400 g)

 BE CAREFUL! HAVE A GROWN-UP HELP YOU DO THIS.

GET THIS:

3 cups (600 g) sugar

1 cup (240 ml) water

A few drops of food coloring (optional)

½ teaspoon flavoring oil or extract, like mint, cinnamon, vanilla, or lemon (optional)

Saucepan

Wooden mixing spoon

Wooden skewer that's taller than your jar (below)

A thick square of cardboard that will cover the top of the jar

Large (1 quart/1 L), clean glass jar

Oven mitts

DO THIS:

MAKE A BATCH OF SUGAR SYRUP

1. Combine the sugar and water in the saucepan.
2. Bring the mixture to a boil over medium heat, stirring constantly with the wooden spoon until the sugar is completely dissolved and the mixture looks clear. BE CAREFUL! THIS MIX CAN STICK AND BURN!
3. Take the syrup off the heat and stir in any food coloring or flavoring you like.
4. Set the pan aside and let the syrup cool for 10 minutes.

"SEED" YOUR SKEWER AND SET UP YOUR JAR

1. Poke the skewer through the middle of the cardboard square, and then set the assembly back into the jar. The skewer should sit about 1 inch (2.5 cm) inside the jar without touching the sides or bottom.
2. Once you have everything set up, dip the pointy end of the skewer (the end that will be inside the jar) into the hot sugar syrup, pull it out, and then set it back in the jar. Let the sugar-soaked skewer dry inside the jar as the syrup continues to cool on the stove.

(continued)

START GROWING YOUR CRYSTALS

1. When your syrup has cooled for a while and the sugar on your skewer has dried, carefully lift the cardboard and skewer, pour the syrup into the jar, and set the cardboard back in place, so the skewer is immersed in the syrup.

2. Using oven mitts to protect your hands (the syrup might still be pretty warm), move the jar to a safe place so it won't be disturbed—then watch, and wait. Small crystals of rock candy will start to form immediately, but it will take 4 or 5 days for those big, chunky crystals to be ready to "harvest." How long can you wait?

 HOW DID THAT HAPPEN? *When you soaked the skewer in the syrup and then let it dry, tiny crystals of sugar got stuck on the skewer's rough wooden edges. As it sat in the syrup-filled jar, that crust of sugar acted like tiny seeds, giving the larger sugar crystals something to grow on. The crystals grew because the syrup you made was supersaturated—that is, it had more molecules of sugar in it than the cooling water could hold. As the water cooled and evaporated, the sugar began sticking to the seed crystals, making them larger and larger, until they made big blocks of crystal sugar: rock candy. In fact, a few inches of rock candy is likely to contain more than a quadrillion (1,000,000,000,000,000) molecules of sugar.*

FIVE-MINUTE ICE CREAM

You certainly don't need to know how to make ice cream to enjoy it. But knowing how to shake up a batch of your favorite flavor, and understanding what's going on when you do that, can help you appreciate the work and know-how that goes into making some of the delicious foods we're lucky enough to be able to pick up, ready-made, at the grocery store. It seems like freezing sweetened cream into ice cream would be pretty easy, but it turns out that cream is complex stuff made from a delicate balance of fat, protein, and water. When you freeze cream, the water gets solid first and the whole thing breaks apart. In order to keep it creamy, you've got to keep it moving. So get shaking!

YOWZA!

YUM!

EASY-PEASY

LESS THAN 30 MINUTES

GATHER AT HOME

LESS THAN $5

SAFE

Makes 1 large or 2 small dishes of ice cream

GET THIS:

Enough ice to fill a gallon-sized zipper-lock
  plastic bag
6 tablespoons (110 g) coarse salt, like kosher
  salt or rock salt, plus a pinch
1 tablespoon (15 g) sugar
½ cup (120 ml) half-and-half
2 tablespoons (30 ml) chocolate syrup (optional)
½ teaspoon flavor extract, like vanilla,
  strawberry, maple, or mint

Gallon-sized zipper-lock plastic bag
Large bowl
Pint-sized zipper-lock plastic bag
Big dish towel or small bath towel (optional)

DO THIS:

MAKE YOUR ICE COLDER THAN COLD

1. Fill the gallon bag about halfway with ice cubes.
2. Add the 6 tablespoons (10 g) salt and shake the bag so the salt gets all over the ice. Stand the bag in the bowl to keep it from falling over while you mix up the ice cream.

MAKE THE ICE-CREAM BASE

1. Put the half-and-half, chocolate syrup (if you want), sugar, extract, and pinch of salt in the pint-size bag.
2. Seal the bag perfectly shut. (Any gaps in the seal and you'll make a mess instead of ice cream.)

SHAKE YOUR BOOTY!

1. Put the small bag of ice-cream base into the big bag of ice and gently push it down so the ice completely surrounds the ice cream.
2. Seal the big bag.

(continued)

3. If you want, you can wrap the towel around the whole thing. Then pick it up and shake hard for about 5 minutes. If you don't mind getting your hands cold, just grab the bag and have at it! Unless you've been training for the Ice Cream Olympics (that's not real, but wouldn't it be cool if it was?), you'll probably need to take a break after a few minutes, or pass it off to a friend to shake for a while.

DIG IN!

1. Open up the big bag and take out the small bag of ice cream, which should now be creamy and thick.
2. Wipe all the salt and water off the ice-cream bag and open it up. Dig in and get happy!

HOW DID THAT HAPPEN? *Ice cream is made of three things: ice, cream, and air. Ice makes it thick. Cream makes it tasty. But air is what makes it feel creamy on your tongue. Here's how it works...*

When a mixture of cream, sugar, and flavoring is frozen, the water in the cream freezes into ice crystals, turning the mixture from liquid to solid. The size of the ice crystals determines whether the results are smooth or grainy. Shaking the mixture as the ice forms breaks the crystals into small pieces and traps air into the mix. Those tiny pockets of air keep the crystals separate from one another, so the base of sugar and cream doesn't ever freeze as solid as the water in the mix. Instead, it keeps flowing, making the ice cream feel creamy and smooth in your mouth. Trapping air in the freezing mixture also makes the ice cream fluffier, and easier to scoop and bite into.

PS: *If you're wondering why you added salt to the bag of ice before you shook up your ice cream, it's because melted salt water is actually colder than solid ice water. The only way to freeze ice cream is to make sure the ice around it is colder than the ice inside it!*

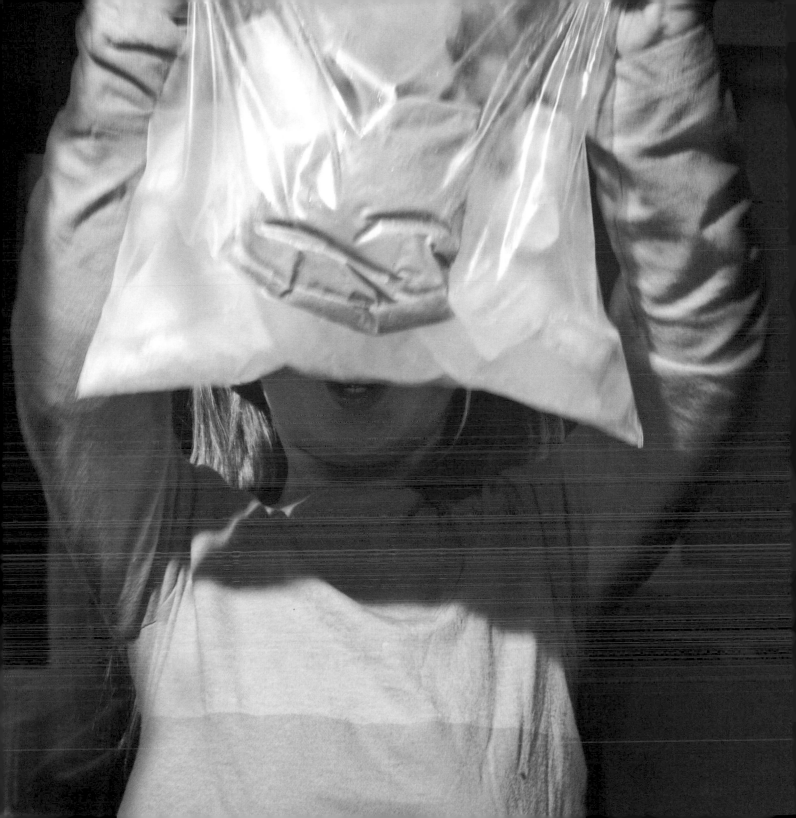

CREAMLESS ICE CREAM

This "ice cream" doesn't use cream. In fact, it's totally dairy free—and practically fat free. And there's no sugar! The secret ingredient is bananas. Bananas store their energy in the form of starch and convert that starch to sugar as they ripen. The change is awesome. A mature banana that's yellow, but still green at the ends, has 25 parts starch to 1 part sugar. Wait a day or two until you can see brown stripes on the banana's skin and everything will have switched. The banana is now 1 part starch to about 20 parts sugar. The fruit inside will be smooth, creamy, fragrant and so-o-o-o-o sweet!

COOL

YUM!

EASY-PEASY

LESS THAN 30 MINUTES

GATHER AT HOME

LESS THAN $5

SAFE

Makes about 2 cups (480 ml)

GET THIS:

4 very ripe (but not overripe!) bananas, peeled, broken into chunks, and frozen solid
Pinch of ground cinnamon
½ teaspoon vanilla extract

Blender
Rubber spatula
Container with a cover to store any uneaten portions

DO THIS:

SMASH IT ALL TOGETHER...

1. Put everything in the blender and blend until smooth.
2. Start on the slowest speed and work up to the fastest, using the tamper to help everything blend smoothly.
3. Reduce the speed of the blender to the lowest level before turning it off.

...AND ENJOY!

1. Scrape into bowls with the rubber spatula and dig in!
2. You can keep this tasty treat in the freezer for up to about 2 hours. After that it will start to freeze solid and will need to be chopped up and run through a blender again.

HOW DID THAT HAPPEN? *Unripe bananas are rich in starches that turn into sugar as the fruit ripens. At the same time, enzymes in the fruit soften the fruit's fibers, turning them creamy. The combination of high sugar concentration and creamy mouthfeel makes a puréed frozen banana a dead ringer for sweet, rich, ice cream.*

SWEET LAVA

Cook caramel sugar syrup, aerate it with the same acid-base reaction (vinegar and baking soda) that makes science-fair volcanoes erupt, and create an explosion of taste! It looks like hardened magma, but tastes like candy. Note: While this candy is in its molten state, it doesn't just *look* like lava, it *burns* like lava, so be careful. When you add the baking soda, the lava will foam up; carefully pour it into your prepared pan and don't touch it. Step away and let it cool like the lava field it resembles. Once it's solid, it will be safe to touch.

Makes about 1 pound (455 g)

 BE CAREFUL! HAVE A GROWN-UP HELP YOU DO THIS.

CRAZY!

YUM!

A LITTLE HELP, PLEASE!

30–60 MINUTES

GATHER AT HOME

LESS THAN $5

BE CAREFUL

GET THIS:

Nonstick cooking spray

1 cup (200 g) sugar

1 cup (240 ml) dark corn syrup

2 tablespoons (30 ml) white vinegar

1 tablespoon (14 g) baking soda

9-by-13-inch (23-by-33-cm) baking pan

Large sheet of aluminum foil

Medium saucepan

Mixing spoon

Candy thermometer or high-temp instant-read thermometer

Oven mitts

DO THIS:

PREPARE THE PAN

1. Line the baking pan with the aluminum foil.
2. Spray the foil with oil.

COOK THE CANDY

1. Stir the sugar, corn syrup, and vinegar together in the saucepan.
2. Cook over medium heat, stirring all the time, until the mixture is boiling rapidly and registers 310°F (155°C) on the candy or instant-read thermometer. (Make sure the point of the thermometer doesn't touch the pan or you won't get an accurate reading.)

MAKE IT FOAM

1. Remove the saucepan from the heat and put it on a heat-resistant surface, like a stone or tile counter.
2. Stir in the baking soda. The mixture will immediately foam up.
3. Pour the candy into the prepared baking pan, but don't try to spread it out or you'll deflate it. Don't worry if the candy doesn't flow all the way to the edges of the pan.
4. Let cool until firm, about 30 minutes. Break into bite-size pieces and enjoy!

(continued)

HOW DID THAT HAPPEN? *Chemically, all foods are either acids or bases. The difference has to do with their electrical charge. Acidic foods, which are positively charged, give off hydrogen ions (H+) when dissolved in liquid. Base foods, which are negatively charged, give off hydroxide ions (OH-).*

In this experiment, you mix together an acid (vinegar) and a base (baking soda, or sodium bicarbonate). The two ingredients combine in a chemical reaction that neutralizes both, producing a mixture that has no electrical charge. The neutral by-products that come out of the reaction are water, sodium acetate (a salt), and carbon dioxide. The water evaporates, the salt hangs around and balances the sweet flavor of the sugar in the mixture, and the carbon dioxide, which is a gas, gets trapped in the thick sugar syrup, causing it to bubble up and aerate.

The result is a block of sugar crystals that have been puffed up and punctured by zillions of air bubbles. Because the air interrupts the crystallization of the sugar syrup, the texture of the finished candy is more like a chunk of Styrofoam than a cube of caramel. The hard sugar crunch is still there but the crystal structure has been inflated like a bunch of balloons. When you take a bite, the tissue-thin crystal walls crack between your teeth, the air escapes, and the foam deflates. You feel like you're biting into a chewy piece of sponge, but it's the same hard crystal structure as the Rock Candy on page 45. You're feeling the awesome power of air once again!

POPPING PEBBLES

These candies are like the Pop Rocks you buy at the store. They're made by trapping carbon dioxide in a sugar syrup. Most of us don't have the pressure chamber needed to force the gas into the syrup and keep it there (the way the store-bought candies are made), so we have to use chemistry instead. The finished candy pebbles are not quite as incendiary as the factory-produced poppers, but they're pretty cool (and wildly tickly on the tongue). And you made them yourself, which is a whole other level of awesome.

YOWZA!

YUM!

A LITTLE HELP, PLEASE!

30–60 MINUTES

GO SHOP

LESS THAN $5

BE CAREFUL

Makes about 3 cups (600 g)

 BE CAREFUL! HAVE A GROWN-UP HELP YOU DO THIS.

GET THIS:

1 cup (100 g) powdered sugar

2 teaspoons (9 g) citric acid (sour salt)

2 cups (400 g) granulated sugar

½ cup (120 ml) light corn syrup

¼ cup (60 ml) water

½ teaspoon flavor extract, like lemon, vanilla, cinnamon, or raspberry

1 teaspoon baking soda

Rimmed cookie sheet

Medium saucepan

Mixing spoon

Pastry brush and a glass of water

Candy thermometer or high-temp instant-read thermometer

Gallon-sized zipper-lock plastic bag

Hammer or meat pounder

(continued)

DO THIS:

PREPARE THE PAN
1. Spread the powdered sugar over the bottom of the cookie sheet.
2. Sprinkle half of the citric acid on top.

COOK THE CANDY
1. Combine the granulated sugar, corn syrup, water, and remaining citric acid in the saucepan and stir until all of the sugar is moistened.
2. Cook over medium heat, stirring all the time, until the mixture is boiling rapidly, and then stop stirring. BE CAREFUL! THIS MIX CAN STICK AND BURN!
3. Using the pastry brush dipped in the glass of water, brush water on any sugar syrup that splashed onto the sides of the saucepan, making sure there are no undissolved sugar crystals in the pan.
4. Boil without stirring until the mixture registers 305°F (151°C) on the candy or instant-read thermometer dipped into the center of the syrup. (Make sure the point of the thermometer doesn't touch the pan or you won't get an accurate reading.)

MAKE IT POP
1. Remove the pan from the heat and put it on a heat-resistant surface, like a stone or tile counter, or on a pot holder. Wait 3 to 5 minutes, until the syrup has cooled to about 275°F (135°C).
2. Stir in the extract and baking soda. The mixture will immediately foam up. Stir until everything is well combined.
3. Pour the candy onto the powdered sugar in the prepared cookie sheet. Don't be concerned about filling the pan or getting an even layer. The candy will naturally form globs and lumps in the pan.

BANG IT!
1. Let the candy cool until solid and cool enough to touch, about 30 minutes.
2. Lift the candy from the cookie sheet and break into big pieces. Put in the zipper-lock bag, squeeze out the excess air, and seal the bag.
3. Bang the candy into bite-size pieces with the hammer or the flat side of the meat pounder. (Don't pulverize it! You want chunks, not powder.) Now it's ready to eat.
4. Store any extra pebbles in an airtight container to keep them dry so they don't lose their pop!

(continued)

HOW DID THAT HAPPEN? *The science of getting gas into candy works like the acid-base reaction in Sweet Lava (see page 56), but there's also crystal science going on here.*

When you boil sugar syrup for candy, you have to be precise about tracking its temperature. That's because the temperature of boiling sugar syrup is a way to measure the exact amount of water and sugar in the mixture.

Plain water boils at 212°F (100°C). When you dissolve sugar in water, the mixture needs to get hotter to reach a boil (to find out what happens when water boils, see below). The higher the percentage of sugar to water, the hotter it has to get to keep boiling. For example, a syrup that is 40 percent sugar and 60 percent water boils at 214°F (101°C). Syrup that is 80 percent sugar and 20 percent water boils at 234°F (112°C). That means you can tell the amount of sugar in a sugary syrup by taking its temperature.

As the syrup in our candy boiled, the water in it evaporated. The longer it boiled, the more the amount of water in the syrup diminished and the percentage of sugar grew. As that happened, the mixture had to get hotter to maintain a boil. By the time the boiling point reached 300°F (150°C), the syrup was almost all sugar, about 98 percent, and only 2 percent remained as water.

At that concentration, if a sugar crystal happened to drop into the syrup, it would trigger a chain reaction, crystallizing all the sugar in the syrup and making it turn solid—which is what happens when you make Rock Candy (page 45). That's why you used a pastry brush dipped in water to wash any undissolved sugar crystals into the syrup. If even one crystal fell in when it was getting hot enough to solidify, the whole thing would have turned into a pot of crunchy crystals, rather than a smooth, hard candy.

how to boil water

As a pot of water heats, the water molecules near the bottom of the pot warm up first. As they get hotter, they move faster. Eventually, they move fast enough to rise toward the surface of the water, where they displace the cooler molecules up above, forcing them to fall to the bottom of the pot, where they in turn are heated and begin to rise.

Eventually, the water gets hot enough to turn the water molecules at the bottom of the pot into steam. Because steam is less dense than water, it rises, causing the surface of the water to swirl. This slight movement on the surface of the water is the visual sign that the water is between 170° and 180°F (77° and 82°C).

When enough steam forms, bubbles at the edge of the pot begin to break through the surface into a simmer, at about 190°F (88°C). When bubbles undulate across the entire surface of the water, it's said to be at a gentle boil, or about 210°F (99°C). In just 1 or 2 more degrees, the surface of the water will break into large, vigorous bubbles. This stage is called a "rolling boil."

CANDY-CANE ORIGAMI

Candy canes come bent, so it's no big deal to bend them some more. And when you do, you're experiencing the near-infinite possibilities of manipulating sugar to your every whim. Candy canes are made from granulated sugar and corn syrup. Both are technically sucrose, a common sugar made from a molecule of fructose and a molecule of glucose, but the corn syrup has more fructose, which means the sugar crystals in the candy cane don't fit tightly together. The crystals have space between them, which allows them to bend and move without cracking.

Makes 10 candies (or as many as you like!)

 BE CAREFUL! HAVE A GROWN-UP HELP YOU DO THIS.

COOL

YUM!

A LITTLE HELP, PLEASE!

LESS THAN 30 MINUTES

GO SHOP

LESS THAN $5

BE CAREFUL

GET THIS:

10 candy canes or candy sticks (or as many as you like)

Sheet of heavy-duty aluminum foil, or regular foil folded into a 3-ply piece

Cookie sheet

Wire cooling rack

DO THIS:

GET EVERYTHING READY

1. Preheat the oven to 250°F (120°C).
2. Line the cookie sheet with the aluminum foil.
3. Arrange the candy canes on the foil, but make sure none of the pieces are touching.

HEAT UP THE CANDY CANES...

1. Bake for about 10 minutes, or until the candy is pliable.
2. Let a grown-up test how hot the candy canes are before you pick them up. They have to be a little hot—about as hot as hot tap water—in order to be soft enough to bend.

...AND PLAY!

1. When you get the okay, lift up a piece of candy and play! You can stretch it, twist it, bend it into shapes, tie it into knots, or roll it into balls, whatever you want.
2. Work quickly! In about a minute, the candy will set up and become unbendable again. If you are still working on a twist or shape, you can put it back into the hot oven for another minute or so and it will become pliable again.

(continued)

HOW DID THAT HAPPEN? *An ice cube is made up of water molecules locked into uniform, rigid crystals. All the molecules are the same, so they can lock together into a rigid structure. But add heat, and the molecules start to move. That movement breaks everything apart and the molecules separate into liquid water.*

That's essentially what's happening here. But unlike ice, the molecules in a candy cane are not all the same. They have several different shapes, so when they solidify, the solid is more like a jumbled-up tangle than an organized crystal. As the candy heats and the molecules start to move around, instead of changing form, the solid candy gets floppy without melting into a liquid. That's when you can bend it and reform it into new shapes.

CHAPTER 3

COOKIES, CAKES, AND OTHER BAKED EXPERIMENTS

People often say that cooking is an art and baking is a science. What they mean is that when you're baking, you need to measure precisely and follow recipes exactly; but when you're cooking, you don't have to be that exact. (Throw a few more ounces of meat in the stew you're cooking and you just have a meatier stew, but add another teaspoon of baking soda to the cake you're baking—and you have an eruption!)

In fact, so much of successful baking is dependent on scientific principles that you can use almost any baking recipe as a mini science experiment. You can't bake a simple yeast bread, like English muffins, without noticing that yeast is a living organism, and keeping it alive is what makes your muffins puff. You can't aerate a sponge cake without learning that heat makes air expand, and you can't dip into an old-fashioned pudding cake, with its bottom layer of rich chocolate goo, without wondering how the heck that happened.

IN THIS CHAPTER:

MOON-CYCLE COOKIES

DISAPPEARING PEPPERMINT PILLOWS

MILE-HIGH POPOVERS

40-SECOND SPONGE CAKE

MAKE-YOUR-OWN ENGLISH MUFFINS

MOLTEN CHOCOLATE CUPCAKES

FLIP-FLOPPING PUDDING CAKE

BIZARRO BROWNIES

MOON-CYCLE COOKIES

The design of these cookies comes from old-time astronomical charts that depict the phases of the moon. By watching the moon and observing how its shape changed from day to day, early scientists figured out the moon's orbit around Earth. These cookies connect us to those early scientists, but they do it in a way that's pretty cool—making cookie dough bake up light or dark simply by changing the amount of baking soda in the recipe. Usually, baking soda is added to cakes, muffins, and biscuits to make them rise, but when you see baking soda in a cookie recipe, that's not the main reason it's there—it's to make them brown.

Makes 18 cookies

 BE CAREFUL! HAVE A GROWN-UP HELP YOU DO THIS.

GET THIS:

1 stick (½ cup/110 g) unsalted butter, at
  room temperature
1 cup (200 g) sugar
1 teaspoon (5 ml) vanilla extract
½ teaspoon salt
1 large egg
2¼ cups (285 g) unbleached all-purpose flour,
  plus extra for dusting
½ teaspoon cream of tartar
½ teaspoon baking soda
2 tablespoons (30 ml) milk

2 cookie sheets
Aluminum foil, parchment paper, or
  silicone baking pads
Butter knife
Measuring cups and spoons
3 bowls
Electric mixer or wooden mixing spoon
Rubber spatula
Sticky notes, masking tape and pen, or other
  way to mark the bowls
Mixing spoons
Rolling pin
Small spatula

(continued)

CRAZY!

EAT UP!

A LITTLE HELP, PLEASE!

AFTERNOON PROJECT

GATHER AT HOME

LESS THAN $5

SOME COOKING

DO THIS:

GET THE OVEN HOT AND THE PAN READY

1. Preheat the oven to 350°F (180°C).
2. Line the 2 cookie sheets with the aluminum foil, parchment paper, or silicone baking pads.

MAKE TWO COOKIE DOUGHS

1. Cut the butter into small pieces and mix with the sugar, vanilla, and salt in a bowl.
2. Beat until soft using the electric mixer or by hand with the wooden spoon.
3. Beat in the egg until smooth, scraping the bowl with the rubber spatula as needed. Set aside.
4. Use the sticky notes, tape and pen, or other method to mark the remaining 2 clean bowls with the words "Light" and "Dark" (or draw an open circle for the light dough and a filled-in circle for the dark dough). The light-colored dough (for the light side of the moon) goes in the "Light" bowl; the dark-colored dough (for the dark side of the moon) goes in the "Dark" bowl.
5. Put 1 cup plus 2 tablespoons (140 g) of the flour in each bowl. Put the cream of tartar in the "Light" bowl and the baking soda in the "Dark" bowl.
6. Add half of the butter-sugar-egg mixture to each bowl. Add 1 tablespoon of the milk to each bowl and beat each with a clean mixing spoon into a stiff, smooth dough. If the dough gets too stiff to mix, knead the last bits together with your hands.

ROLL OUT THE DOUGHS

1. Tear off 2 large sheets of parchment paper or foil, or set out 2 clean silicone baking pads.
2. Mark a corner of each one so you'll be able to tell the dark dough from the light dough.
3. Start with the dark dough. Dust one of the sheets lightly with flour. Put the dough on the sheet and pat and roll until the dough is about ¼ inch (6 mm) thick. Cut out circles from the dark dough using a 2- to 3-inch (5- to- 7.5 cm) round cutter. You should get 9 dark-moon circles.
4. Prepare the light dough in the same way. You should get 9 light-moon circles.

MAKE MOONS

1. Cut one of each type of cookie in half. Line up one light-dough half with one dark-dough half and lightly press the seam where they meet so you can't see any open space between them. (Don't worry about sealing the seam; the sides will stick to one another during baking.) You'll end up with 2 cookies, both made with half light and half dark dough. Lift the cookies with the small spatula and slide onto a prepared cookie sheet, about 2 inches (5 cm) apart.
3. Cut a thin slice off one side of two of each type of cookie. Line up the small section of one type of cookie with the large section of the other and lightly press the seam, as you did above. You'll end up with 4 cookies, each made with both dark and light dough. Transfer to a prepared cookie sheet.

(continued)

4. Cut a slice about one-fourth of the way in from one side of two of each type of cookie. Line up the small section of one type of cookie with the large section of the other and lightly press the seam, as you did above. You'll end up with 4 cookies, each made with both dark and light dough. Transfer to a prepared cookie sheet.
5. Cut a slice about one-third of the way in from one side of two of each type of cookie. Line up the small section of one type of cookie with the large section of the other and lightly press the seam, as you did above. You'll end up with 4 cookies, each made with both dark and light dough. Transfer to a prepared cookie sheet.
6. You should have 2 whole cookies of each type left (4 total). Put them on a prepared cookie sheet.

BAKE

1. Bake the cookies, one sheet at a time, for 7 minutes each, or until "Light" cookies are lightly browned.
2. Remove from the oven and let cool for a minute on the pan, then transfer with the spatula to the wire rack to cool to room temperature, about 10 minutes.
3. Set up your cookies (you'll have enough to make 2 full cycles) and eat the moon!

 HOW DID THAT HAPPEN? *Cream of tartar is an acid. Acids inhibit browning. Baking soda is a base. Bases neutralize acids. By mixing cream of tartar into one half of the dough and baking soda into the other, you created one dough that browned and one that didn't. Put them side by side in a cookie and you've got a treat that shows both the dark and light sides of the moon.*

DISAPPEARING PEPPERMINT PILLOWS

COOL

YUM!

PLAN IN ADVANCE

AFTERNOON PROJECT

GATHER AT HOME

LESS THAN $5

SAFE

These melt-in-your-mouth cookies are called meringue (say "ma-RANG"). They're made from just egg whites, sugar—and air. Even though they're sweet, delicious, and look like other cookies, they're little more than sweet shells filled with air. Put one in your mouth, and it will vanish in a peppermint-scented poof! Meringue cookies are unique not just because of what they have in them, but because of what they *don't* have: meringues don't contain flour. Flour is the main structural component of most cookies, giving them their cakey, chewy, flaky deliciousness. But flour doesn't melt in your mouth the way that meringue does, and that's what makes these cookies pretty special.

Makes 24 cookies

GET THIS:

2 large eggs

1 cup (100 g) powdered sugar

⅛ teaspoon cream of tartar (optional)

⅛ teaspoon peppermint extract

1 candy cane, broken in pieces, or 4 peppermint hard candies

Cookie sheet

Parchment paper

Standing mixer with whisk attachment; everything has to be *really* clean

A few small bowls for separating eggs

Small covered container to save egg yolks

Sheet of aluminum foil

Sifter or fine-mesh sieve

Soupspoon

Small spoon

Quart-sized zipper-lock plastic bag

Hammer or meat pounder

(continued)

DO THIS:

GET EVERYTHING READY

1. Preheat the oven to 175°F (80°C).
2. Line the cookie sheet with the parchment paper.
3. Make sure the mixer bowl is squeaky clean. It can't have any greasy stuff in it or on it. If it does, your cookies will fall flat.

SEPARATE THE EGGS

(NOTE: YOU MIGHT WANT SOME ADULT HELP WITH THIS. IT CAN BE KIND OF TRICKY!)

1. Carefully hit one of the eggs on the edge of a small bowl, just hard enough to crack the shell, but not hard enough to smash it.
2. Hold one hand over the bowl with your fingers close together and your palm cupped upward. Gently dump the egg out of its shell into your cupped hand.
3. Spread your fingers slowly. Let the egg white run through your fingers into the small bowl, but keep the yolk in your hand. If the yolk breaks while you're doing this, you'll need to put it away for some other use (maybe scrambled eggs for breakfast?). Clean your hands and the small bowl, and start again.
4. When all the white from the first egg is safely in the small bowl, pour it into the big bowl of your stand mixer. Put the yolk into a container nearby. Then repeat with the other egg and another small bowl. Don't let any egg yolk get into the mixing bowl! (Using the small bowls first helps you avoid ruining a whole batch of egg whites.)
5. Cover the egg yolks and store in the refrigerator for another use. Mayo Shake (page 135) calls for a whole egg. They'll keep for up to 3 days.

SIFT THE SUGAR

1. Put the foil on the counter or on a table.
2. Sift the powdered sugar onto the foil or tap it through the sieve to get out any lumps.

BEAT THE EGG WHITES

1. Using the whisk attachment on your mixer, beat the egg whites and cream of tartar, if using, on medium speed until they're foamy. (Cream of tartar is a mild acid that will help the protein in the egg whites coagulate faster and last longer.)
2. Turn the mixer speed up to medium-high and beat the egg whites until they're white and thick, but still soft—sort of like hand cream.
3. With the mixer still on, use the soupspoon to add the sifted sugar to the egg whites a couple of spoonfuls at a time.

4. When all the sugar has been mixed in, add the peppermint extract. The mixture will look bright white, smooth, and shiny.

MAKE THE COOKIES

1. Using the small spoon, plop the egg white mixture onto the parchment in blobs about the size of golf balls. Put them just far enough apart so that they don't touch.

CRUSH THE CANDY

1. Put the candy in the zipper-lock plastic bag. Press out the extra air and seal the bag.
2. Bang the candy with the hammer or the flat side of the meat pounder until it's broken into a rough powder.
3. Sprinkle the crushed candy over the cookies.

BAKE

1. Put the sheet of cookies into the preheated oven and bake until they're firm and dry, about 3 hours.
2. Turn off the oven and let them sit in the oven for another hour.
3. Remove from the parchment paper and eat up.

HOW DID THAT HAPPEN? *Egg whites are just protein and water. When you beat an egg white, the liquid protein molecules separate into strings and get tangled up, trapping air and water in an interlocking web of tiny protein bubbles. The more air that's beaten in, the more the egg-white bubbles inflate. Water helps keep the walls of the inflating bubbles moist and flexible, but at a certain point, those walls can't stretch anymore. Like balloons blown to their limit, the bubbles start to pop, releasing air and water. Then the whole network collapses. By adding sugar, you keep that from happening. Sugar holds on to water.*

When you make meringues, you start by beating the egg whites without any sugar. That gives the protein strings the best chance to form bonds with each other, tangle up, and trap air. When the egg whites are full of air, but still have enough water to keep them soft, you add the sugar. The sugar bonds with the water, keeping the bubble walls moist and flexible so they can expand more without bursting. In that way, you get the lightest possible meringue.

Because meringue cookies don't contain flour, they really don't need to bake to get crispy. Instead, they just need to dry out. That's why you heat them at a low temperature for a long time. The protein bubbles hold onto the air, but the water evaporates, leaving behind a dry, crisp network of air bubbles that miraculously dissolves when it hits the moisture inside your mouth.

MILE-HIGH POPOVERS

Popovers are crisp and soft, buttery brown, and completely hollow, so they're great for filling. Some people like to fill them with gravy; others are partial to strawberry jam. How they get to be so delicious and so, well, empty, is pure science. Popover batter is very similar to the batter used to make crepes (paper-thin French pancakes), which is almost equal parts of flour, egg, and milk. In a crepe, the thin skin is wrapped around a filling. In a popover, the batter is baked in muffin tins and the skin is more like a balloon than a wrapper. When they come out of the oven, your popovers are all going to be slightly different shapes, because the ones on the outside of the muffin pan get more heat than the ones in the center, and they all puff up differently.

COOL

YUM!

A LITTLE HELP, PLEASE!

30–60 MINUTES

GATHER AT HOME

LESS THAN $5

SOME COOKING

Makes 8 popovers

 BE CAREFUL! HAVE A GROWN-UP HELP YOU DO THIS.

GET THIS:

3 tablespoons (45 g) butter, melted

1 cup (240 ml) milk

2 extra-large eggs

1 tablespoon (15 g) sugar

1 cup (125 g) all-purpose flour

½ teaspoon salt, if using unsalted butter

Your favorite filling, such as PB&J, mashed-up
banana, jelly, gravy, guacamole, or tuna (optional)

Muffin tin

Pastry brush

Microwave-safe glass measuring cup

Microwave oven

Blender

Oven mitts

DO THIS:

GET OVEN AND PAN HOT

1. Preheat the oven to 400°F (200°C).
2. Using 1 tablespoon of the melted butter, brush 8 muffin cups to coat the bottom and sides with butter and put the pan in the oven for at least 5 minutes while you make the batter.

BLEND BATTER

1. Warm the milk in the microwave-safe cup in the microwave for 30 seconds.
2. Put the eggs and sugar in the blender and blend until light yellow, about 10 seconds.
3. Add the warm milk and blend.
4. Add the flour, the remaining melted butter, and the salt, if using, and blend until the batter is smooth and foamy.

(continued)

BAKE RIGHT AWAY

1. Using the oven mitts, pull the muffin tin from the oven.
2. Working quickly so the pan doesn't cool too much, pour the batter about two-thirds of the way up each of the buttered muffin cups.
3. Bake until puffed and golden, about 30 minutes.

OBSERVE AND DIG IN

1. Carefully remove the popovers from the pan. Tear one open (be careful of the steam!). What's inside? Right. Absolutely nothing.
2. Add your favorite filling and dig in!

 HOW DID THAT HAPPEN? *The blender forces a lot of air into the popover batter. When you pour it into the hot muffin tin, the surface of the batter sets up right away. The air bubbles are now trapped. As they heat, the expanding bubbles bump into each other, combining into one big bubble with a liquid-batter balloon around it. As the popovers bake, the batter solidifies around an empty center. If the pan isn't hot when the batter goes in, the balloon never forms, the air doesn't get trapped, and your popover won't pop!*

40-SECOND SPONGE CAKE

WOW!

YUM!

A LITTLE HELP, PLEASE!

LESS THAN 30 MINUTES

GATHER AT HOME

LESS THAN $10

BE CAREFUL

Most cakes bake in an oven for 40 minutes or more, but here's one that takes just 40 seconds—and it's as light and airy as any long-rising cake. The trick is using a whipped-cream siphon to get air into the batter before you start baking, and then baking it in a microwave instead of a standard oven.

Whipped-cream siphons are pricey, usually costing about $100. If you don't already have one, that's a lot to spend on sponge cake, even a mind-boggling cake like this one. Once you have the siphon, it can, obviously, be used for making whipped cream. And this kind of siphon is also the tool that high-end chefs use for making spectacular foams from all sorts of wacky ingredients, from abalone to zucchini.

Makes 4 individual cakes

 BE CAREFUL! HAVE A GROWN-UP HELP YOU DO THIS.

GET THIS:

6 tablespoons (85 g) unsalted butter

4 large eggs

¼ cup (50 g) sugar

¼ teaspoon salt

¼ cup (60 ml) half-and-half

½ cup (100 g) all-purpose flour

1 tablespoon (15 g) unsweetened cocoa powder

Nonstick cooking spray

½ cup (120 ml) chocolate syrup

4 large, ripe strawberries

Small saucepan

Big bowl

Large wire whisk (the bigger the better)

1-pint (480 ml) whipping siphon, like the iSi Gourmet Whip

2 nitrous oxide (N_2O/whipped cream) cartridges

Four 7-ounce (210-ml) wax-coated paper cups

1 push pin

Microwave oven

DO THIS:

COOK THE BUTTER UNTIL BROWN

1. Put the butter in the small saucepan and heat over medium heat, stirring or swirling the pan occasionally until the butter stops foaming and starts to turn brown, about 5 minutes. Remove from the heat and let cool.

MAKE THE CAKE BATTER

1. Put the eggs, sugar and salt in the big bowl. Using the wire whisk, mix everything together as fast as you can, until the mixture is thick and changes from deep yellow to light yellow.
2. Mix in the half-and-half, then the flour and cocoa, and then the browned butter, just until the batter is very smooth and uniform in color.

AERATE THE BATTER

1. Pour the batter into the canister of your siphon. Seal the siphon and charge it with two whipped cream (N_2O, not CO_2) cartridges, according to the manufacturer's instructions.
2. Shake up the siphon as hard as you can, until your arms are too tired to shake it anymore.

"BAKE" THE CAKE

1. Poke 3 holes around the sides of each of the 4 paper cups using the push pin. Spray the insides of the cups with the cooking spray.
2. Hold the siphon upside down and insert the nozzle into a prepared cup. Slowly press the handle and move the siphon in a circular motion to evenly fill the cup about one-third of the way up.
3. Put the cup in the microwave and cook on high for about 40 seconds, or until the cake is fluffy and rises to the top of the cup.
4. Invert the cup onto a plate and let stand for at least 1 minute. Fill the rest of the cups and bake one at a time. Remove the cups and discard when all the cakes are done.
5. Drizzle 2 tablespoons of the chocolate syrup over and around each cake and decorate with a strawberry.
6. Serve right away.

HOW DID THAT HAPPEN? *Hot gases make baked goods rise. That gas can be carbon dioxide, created when yeast or baking powder is in the dough, or plain old air from when beaten egg whites are folded into a batter. In this cake, the gas is forced into the cake by putting the batter in a pressurized container called a siphon.*

If you have a SodaStream machine at home, then you've used a carbon-dioxide (CO_2) siphon to make soda. This cake uses a nitrous oxide (N_2O) siphon, which is the kind for making whipped cream. Nitrous oxide dissolves in fat (carbon dioxide doesn't), so when you dispense the fatty cake batter from the nitrous-oxide siphon, it's infused with thousands of gas bubbles. In the microwave, the gas bubbles heat up, getting bigger and bigger, and making the cake rise. When it comes out, the cake sinks back down a little as the gas cools and contracts.

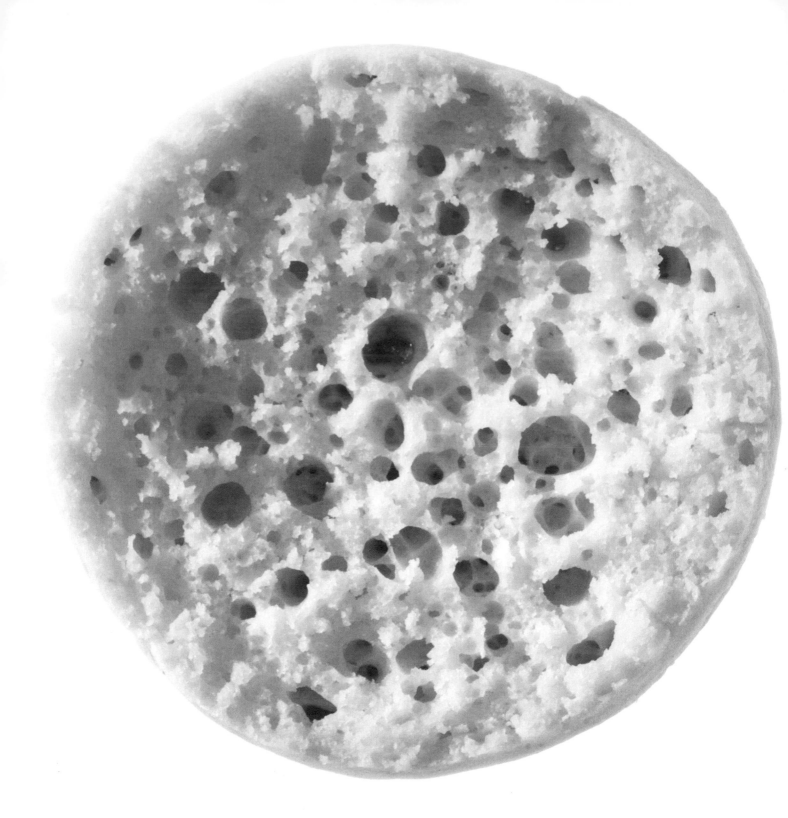

MAKE-YOUR-OWN ENGLISH MUFFINS

For most people, English muffins are something you buy in a store. But before there were big factories making millions of muffins packed with billions of nooks and crannies, people always made English muffins at home. The reason is simple: they're really easy to make—and, as breads go, they're pretty fast, too.

YOWZA!

YUM!

A LITTLE HELP, PLEASE!

30–60 MINUTES

GO SHOP

LESS THAN $5

BE CAREFUL

Makes 8 muffins

 BE CAREFUL! HAVE A GROWN-UP HELP YOU DO THIS.

GET THIS:

1 envelope (¼ oz/2¼ teaspoons) instant yeast

4 teaspoons (20 g) sugar, and a pinch for the yeast

1⅓ cup (315 ml) warm water

1 cup (240 ml) hot water

½ cup (35 g) powdered milk

1 teaspoon salt

1 tablespoon (15 g) vegetable shortening, like Crisco

2 cups (255 g) all-purpose flour

Nonstick cooking spray

Butter and jelly for slathering

Big bowl

Wooden mixing spoon

Clean kitchen towel or plastic wrap

Griddle

Four 3-inch (7.5-cm) muffin rings, or 4 clean tuna-fish cans with their tops, bottoms, and labels removed (look for cans that have a seamed edge on the bottom; some don't and are hard to remove with a can opener)

Cookie sheet

Oven mitts

Spatula or kitchen tongs

Wire cooling rack

Fork

(continued)

DO THIS:

ACTIVATE THE YEAST

1. Mix the yeast, the warm water, and the pinch of sugar in the mixing bowl.
2. Set aside until the yeast is slightly foamy and smells yeasty, about 5 minutes.

MAKE THE DOUGH

1. Add the hot water, the powdered milk, the 4 teaspoons sugar, ½ teaspoon of the salt, and the shortening.
2. Stir until the shortening dissolves.
3. Add the flour and beat with the wooden spoon for 100 strokes. (Are you tired yet?)
4. Cover with the towel or plastic wrap and set aside for 30 minutes until bubbly and foamy.

COOK

1. Stir in the remaining ½ teaspoon salt.
2. Heat the griddle to medium heat, and then coat it with the cooking spray.
3. Spray the insides of the metal rings and place them on the griddle.
4. Fill each ring with a scant ½ cup (120 ml) of batter and cover them all with the cookie sheet.
5. Cook until the muffins are set on the bottom and browned, about 5 minutes.
6. Using your oven mitts, remove the cookie sheet. Then flip each ring with the spatula, or turn them with your kitchen tongs. Cover again and cook for another 5 minutes, or until well browned on both sides.
7. Using the oven mitts or tongs, transfer the muffins to the wire rack to cool. Carefully remove the rings (ASK AN ADULT TO HELP YOU DO THIS!). Then use the rings to make more English muffins with the remaining batter.

EAT

1. Split the muffins with the fork.
2. Toast and eat with butter and jelly.

 HOW DID THAT HAPPEN? *Ever wonder how all those delicious, butter-soaking nooks and crannies got into your English muffins? It's a combination of gluten (the really chewy elastic protein in bread) and yeast. Gluten forms when you add water to wheat flour. It's a combination of two proteins in wheat that aren't stretchy at all until they get moistened and mixed together.*

Yeasts are microscopic fungi that feed off the sugars in dough. They take in oxygen and produce carbon dioxide, just like you do when you breathe. All you have to do to get nice, puffy, chewy English muffins is build up the gluten (that's why you mix the dough 100 strokes) and take care of the yeast by providing a warm, moist, energy-rich dough to feed it and keep it growing.

MOLTEN CHOCOLATE CUPCAKES

The sweet magma in the center of these indulgent cupcakes is pure dark chocolate mousse (pronounced "moose"). They bake in just 15 minutes. You have to be precise in your timing or the mousse will solidify into fudge. And you have to eat them pretty fast, too, or those moussy centers will turn rock hard as they cool—just like real magma does.

YOWZA!

YUM!

A LITTLE HELP, PLEASE!

LESS THAN 30 MINUTES

GATHER AT HOME

LESS THAN $10

BE CAREFUL

Makes 12 cupcakes

 BE CAREFUL! HAVE A GROWN-UP HELP YOU DO THIS.

GET THIS:

Nonstick cooking spray and a bit of flour for
   the pan
2 sticks (1 cup/220 g) unsalted butter, cut
   into tablespoon-sized pieces
8 ounces (230 g) semisweet chocolate, chopped
¾ cup (150 g) sugar
½ teaspoon vanilla extract
7 large eggs, beaten
Pinch of salt
7 tablespoons (55 g) all-purpose flour

Muffin tin (sorry, but paper muffin cups probably
   won't work for this)
Large, heavy saucepan
Wooden mixing spoon
Wire cooling rack
Thin-bladed knife

DO THIS:

GET THE OVEN AND PAN HOT

1. Preheat the oven to 325°F (165°C).
2. Spray the cups of the muffin tin with the cooking spray and then dust with a little flour. Set aside.

MAKE THE BATTER

1. Melt the butter in the saucepan over medium heat until about half melted, stirring to keep it from browning.
2. Add the chocolate and continue cooking and stirring until half the chocolate is melted.
3. Remove from the heat and continue stirring until everything is melted and smooth.
4. Mix in the sugar, vanilla, eggs, and salt until smooth.
5. Mix in the flour, just until blended.

(continued)

MAKE THE CUPCAKES

1. Ladle the batter into the muffin tin, filling each cup about three-fourths full.
2. Bake for 15 minutes or until the edges are set and the centers are still very wet and sunken. DO NOT OVERBAKE! They may still look underdone, but they aren't. If you bake them until they look fully baked, they'll taste like chocolate hockey pucks.

EAT 'EM AND CELEBRATE!

1. Transfer to the wire rack and let cool in the pan for 3 minutes, no longer. Then run the knife around the edge of each cupcake and carefully remove.
2. Eat while still hot. Don't burn your mouth, but if you wait too long, the centers won't be ooey-gooey delicious!

 HOW DID THAT HAPPEN? *If these were made from a typical cupcake batter, which is about 30 percent flour, the gooey centers would taste awful, like raw, starchy, cake batter. But these cupcakes are only 2 percent flour—more like pudding than cake, so slurping into the ooey-gooey center doesn't taste gross. It tastes rich and creamy and YUM!*

The other YUM! factor in these cupcakes is fat. When a floury batter cooks it gets firm. When a fatty batter cooks it flows. Typically, floury batter that is 30 percent flour is also only 12 percent fat. This batter is nearly 30 percent fat. The result is a cupcake that sets around the edges (similar to a popover) but stays moist and fluid in the center.

FLIP-FLOPPING PUDDING CAKE

CRAZY!

YUM!

A LITTLE HELP, PLEASE!

30-60 MINUTES

GATHER AT HOME

LESS THAN $5

SOME COOKING

Pudding cakes are wild. You top a cake batter with some sort of syrup and then bake it. In the oven, the cake part rises up through the syrup (or maybe it's the syrup that sinks down through the cake...). That exchange gives you a brownie resting on a pool of chocolate pudding. Scoop up some cake with the pudding underneath, and then eat it with a spoon.

Makes 8 servings

 BE CAREFUL! HAVE A GROWN-UP HELP YOU DO THIS.

GET THIS:

Butter for greasing the pan

1 cup (125 g) all-purpose flour

2 teaspoons (7 g) baking powder

½ teaspoon baking soda

¼ teaspoon salt

1 cup (220 g) granulated sugar

Pinch of ground cinnamon

½ cup (50 g) unsweetened cocoa powder

½ cup (120 ml) milk

1 teaspoon (5 ml) vanilla extract

¼ cup (60 ml) vegetable oil

½ cup (100 g) dark brown sugar

¼ cup (60 ml) fruit juice (orange, apple, grape, etc.)

¾ cup (180 ml) boiling water

8-inch (20-cm) square baking pan

Large bowl

Mixing spoon

Wire cooling rack

(continued)

DO THIS:

GET THE OVEN HOT AND THE CAKE PAN READY

1. Preheat the oven to 350°F (180°C).
2. Butter the baking pan.

MIX UP THE BATTER

1. In the bowl, stir together the flour, baking powder, baking soda, salt, ¾ cup (150 g) of the sugar, the cinnamon, and ¼ cup (25 g) of the cocoa powder.
2. Add the milk, vanilla, and oil and stir into a thick batter.
3. Pour the batter into the prepared pan and spread evenly. Sprinkle the top with the brown sugar, the remaining ¼ cup (25 g) cocoa powder, and the remaining ¼ cup (50 g) granulated sugar.
4. Pour the fruit juice and boiling water over all.

BAKE

1. Place in the oven and bake for about 30 minutes, or until the cake is set around the sides and the top is loose and bubbly. Remove from the oven.
2. Transfer to the wire rack and let cool for 10 minutes or more. Slice or scoop to serve.

 HOW DID THAT HAPPEN? *Baking powder is a mixture of baking soda (a base) and a dry acid salt. When it gets wet, the base and the acid combine and become active, producing a little bit of carbon-dioxide gas. When you put the cake in the oven, the heated acid breaks down into a stronger acid that reacts with the baking soda again, creating more gas. All this gas causes the cake batter to get filled with thousands of air bubbles. It becomes lighter than the boiling water sitting on top, and the cake rises up through it. The heavier water sinks to the bottom, drawing with it a lot of the sugar in the batter, and creating a delicious, sweet pudding at the bottom of the cake.*

BIZARRO BROWNIES

COOL

YUM!

A LITTLE HELP, PLEASE!

30–60 MINUTES

GATHER AT HOME

LESS THAN $5

BE CAREFUL

These bizarre brownies are the opposite of what every other brownie tries to be—these babies are as slim as a sheet of paper, and crispy, instead of fat and fudgy.

If you've ever made regular brownies, you might notice that there's one other weird thing about these treats: you don't grease the pan. The proportion of butter to flour is so delicately balanced that any added fat will make the brownies split. Don't worry; they never stick.

Makes 24 brownie-cookies

 BE CAREFUL! HAVE A GROWN-UP HELP YOU DO THIS.

GET THIS:

1 stick (½ cup/110 g) unsalted butter, plus more
   for greasing the pan
1 ounce (30 g) unsweetened chocolate,
   broken into pieces
½ cup (100 g) sugar
¼ teaspoon vanilla extract
1 large or extra-large egg
⅓ cup (40 g) all-purpose flour
½ cup (60 g) ground pecans, almonds,
   or walnuts

Rimmed cookie sheet
Large saucepan
Wire cooling rack

DO THIS:

GET THE OVEN HOT AND THE PAN READY

1. Preheat the oven to 375°F (190°C).
2. Butter the cookie sheet.

MAKE THE BATTER

1. Melt the 1 stick butter in the large saucepan over medium heat.
2. Add the chocolate. Remove from the heat and stir until the chocolate is melted.
3. Stir in the sugar, vanilla, and egg until smooth.
4. Stir in the flour and beat well.

BAKE AND ENJOY!

1. Pour the batter into the prepared cookie sheet. Tilt the pan back and forth, coaxing the batter to flow into a thin, even layer.
2. Scatter the ground nuts evenly over the top.
3. Bake for 10 minutes, or until the batter is just set.
4. Remove from the oven and transfer to the wire rack until crisp, about 20 minutes.
5. Break into 24 rough-shaped pieces (as you would peanut brittle, for example) and crunch away!

HOW DID THAT HAPPEN? *All cakes and cookies are built from the same foundation ingredients: flour, sugar, butter (or shortening), eggs, and sometimes a liquid, like milk. Depending on the ratio of these ingredients to one another, you can end up with a pound cake, a sponge cake, a muffin, a cupcake, a biscuit, a pancake, a popover, a cookie, a piecrust, a doughnut, or an inedible blob—get the idea?*

This experiment makes a flat, crisp "brownie-cookie" by altering the proportions of the ingredients used to make traditional brownies. It works by decreasing the flour (which makes a batter thick and cakey) and egg (which makes a brownie chewy), and increasing the butter, chocolate, and sugar (all of which make the batter thin). Despite the changes, the texture is totally different, but the brownie flavor stays the same—rich and chocolatey.

Flavor (whether a cookie is chocolate or vanilla or strawberry) is the thing most of us use to differentiate one treat from another. But flavor is completely superficial. As long as the ratio of the other ingredients is kept the same, you can flavor a cake or cookie any way you want. You can even put bacon or chili in it, and it won't change the look or feel or structure of the baked good one bit—only its taste.

CHAPTER 4

FRUITASTIC, VEGEDACIOUS EXPERIMENTS

Whenever you eat fruits or vegetables, you're dining on pieces of plants. Sometimes you eat a plant's root. Sometimes you eat its flower, or its leaves, or its seeds, or its stem.

The roots we eat include carrots, beets, turnips, sweet potatoes, radishes, parsnips, turnips, celery roots, and rutabagas. Vegetables that are actually plant stems include celery, fennel, asparagus, broccoli stems, and rhubarb (some people think rhubarb is a fruit, but look closely and you'll see that it's a stem). Potatoes are underground stems called tubers. Onions and garlic are bulbs, another form of underground stem with pulpy leaves attached. The leaves we eat include spinach, cabbage, kale, lettuce, parsley, leeks, and arugula.

Nuts and beans are the most common seeds we eat. Seed vegetables include peanuts, green beans, chickpeas, lentils, snow peas, and lima beans. The part of the plant that holds the seed is a fruit. Some fruits are sweet, like apples, strawberries, and bananas, and some fruits are not, like peppers, squash, and eggplant. We call sweet fruits "fruit," and we call non-sweet fruits "vegetables," but they're actually all fruit. There are only a few vegetables we eat that are flowers, and most of those are flower buds, such as broccoli, cauliflower, artichokes, and squash blossoms.

IN THIS CHAPTER:

DIY SAUERKRAUT

PICKLES FROM SCRATCH

FRUIT TO BOOT LEATHER

WHAT COLOR IS THE CABBAGE?

POLKA-DOT CELERY

NEVER-FEAR ALFREDO

VEGETABLE-DYED EGGS

DIY MICROWAVE POPCORN

MILKING NUTS

easy almond pudding

DIY SAUERKRAUT

YOWZA!

EAT UP!

A LITTLE HELP, PLEASE!

TWO PHASES

GO SHOP

LESS THAN $10

BE CAREFUL

The only difference between cabbage and sauerkraut is salt and time. This experiment and the next one teach you all about fermentation—the action of helpful bacteria that turns salted vegetables into something amazingly delicious. Give the bacteria a good place to grow, and they do all the rest. If you're worried about growing bacteria in your food, you're not alone...many people worry about that. But very few bacteria are actually harmful, and the harmful ones can't live where there's a lot of salt. As long as you use enough salt in your sauerkraut the only bacteria that will grow are the friendly ones that help you digest your food.

Makes about 3 quarts (3L)

 BE CAREFUL! HAVE A GROWN-UP HELP YOU DO THIS.

GET THIS:

2 large heads (about 3 lb/1.4 g each) of
    green cabbage
¼ cup (50 g) coarse salt, like kosher salt

Sharp knife
Food processor
Gallon crock or a big ceramic bowl
Plate that fits into the crock or bowl
Quart jar filled with water and sealed with a lid

DO THIS:

CUT UP THE CABBAGE

1. Remove the loose outer leaves from the cabbage; discard any that are damaged, wilted, or yellowed, and keep any that aren't broken.
2. Wash the cabbage heads and reserved leaves really well with lots of cold water. Wash your hands really well, too.
3. Cut the cabbage heads into wedges and remove the core. Then cut the wedges into big chunks that will fit into the feed tube of the food processor.
4. Set up your food processor with the slicing disk, not the steel blade that you usually use. Turn the processor on. Using the tamper, push the cabbage pieces into the feed tube to slice the cabbage. (Have an adult help you with the slicing, because it can be a little tricky.)
5. When the processor fills up, turn it off and dump the sliced cabbage into your crock.

MIX IN THE SALT

1. Add the salt to the crock. Using your (clean) hands, knead the cabbage and salt until the slices of cabbage become flexible and leak out a lot of their juices.
2. Push down so that all of the cabbage is covered by juice.

3. Cover everything with the reserved leaves.

4. Put the plate that fits inside the crock on top of the cabbage. Put the jar of water on the plate to weigh it down, and keep all of the cabbage submerged under the water.

GET FERMENTING

1. Set the crock aside at room temperature, 68° to 72°F (20° to 22°C). Check every day to make sure mold is not growing. If you do see mold, discard the sauerkraut and start over. In 5 to 7 days, the cabbage should be bubbly. Don't worry if a little brine drips over the top.

2. Carefully move the crock to a cooler place, about 55°F (13°C). A cellar or cool outbuilding works well in the fall or early winter.

TASTE

1. After 2 weeks, the sauerkraut should taste sour and salty. If you want it more sour, wait another week. Fermentation may take up to 5 weeks, depending on temperature.

2. When your sauerkraut is sour enough for you, start eating! Transfer whatever you don't eat right away to a big storage jar or several smaller ones. Put lids on the jars, close tightly, and refrigerate for up to a year.

HOW DID THAT HAPPEN? *Sauerkraut is pretty easy to make. Once you mix the cabbage and salt together, nature does the rest of the work for you. And you might want to say "Thanks," because that work is sort of complicated.*

Inside most vegetables, including cabbage, there are zillions of microbes. (A microbe is anything alive that's too small to see without a magnifying device, like a microscope.) Some of these microbes are benign, which means they don't do anything harmful. Under the right conditions—like in this really salty environment—these benign microbes stop the growth of other harmful microbes that would cause spoilage and disease. They do this by being the first ones to feed off of the natural sugars in the cabbage, and by producing acids and carbon dioxide that the harmful microbes can't stand.

When you see your sauerkraut turning bubbly and sour, you can tell that those good microbes are at work, making your sauerkraut safe and long-lasting, and preserving its nutrition.

PS: *If you're thinking "Yuk!" when you think about bacteria, think again: 99 percent of the bacteria in the world help us. In fact, the lactic-acid-producing bacteria in pickles and sauerkraut are some of the healthiest and most productive we consume.*

PICKLES FROM SCRATCH

Some people like sour-tasting foods and some don't, which makes sense, because sourness sends a signal telling your brain to *watch out*! That's because some sour-tasting things can make you sick (like unripe fruit or the presence of harmful bacteria). But other sour things can make you healthy (like good bacteria or a sour pickle).

Anybody can make pickles by soaking vegetables in something acidic, like vinegar. That may be easy, but it's also kind of boring. You're going to make pickles in a more interesting way—by fermenting them. To ferment pickles, you put cucumbers in a 7-percent salt solution: that's twice as salty as ocean water. Only probiotic ("good for life") bacteria can thrive at that level of salinity, which is why fermented pickles are so good for you.

CRAZY!

YUM!

EASY-PEASY

TWO PHASES

GO SHOP

LESS THAN $5

SAFE

Makes about 1 quart (1 L)

GET THIS:

3 tablespoons (35 grams) kosher salt
1 pound (455 g) small, firm cucumbers
   (not burpless), washed and dried (6 to 8 cukes)
4 garlic cloves, halved if large
½ teaspoon cracked black peppercorns
Pinch of red pepper flakes (optional)

Large glass measuring cup
One 1-quart (1-L) glass jar with a tight-fitting
   lid, like a Mason or Ball jar

DO THIS:

MAKE THE SALTWATER BRINE

1. Put the salt and 1 cup (240 ml) hot tap water in the measuring cup. Stir until dissolved.
2. When completely dissolved, add 1 cup (240 ml) cold tap water.

MAKE THE PICKLES

1. Cut the blossom ends off the cucumbers. The blossom end has a small, round, rough scab. Remove that scab, but as little of the green as possible.
2. Put the cucumbers in the quart jar vertically, so they're standing on end. They should fit tightly, which will help them stay submerged once the brine is added.
3. Fit the garlic cloves around the cucumbers. Sprinkle the black peppercorns and red pepper flakes (if using) on top.
4. Add enough of the saltwater brine to completely cover the cucumbers, leaving about 1 inch (2.5 cm) of space at the top of the jar. (If you have any brine left, save it. You might need it to top off the pickles as they ferment.)
5. Cover the jar with the lid, but do not screw it on tightly.

(continued)

6. Set in a cool room (about 65°F/18°C) for about a week to ferment, out of direct sunlight.

7. As the pickles ferment, bubbles of carbon-dioxide gas will become visible inside the jar. Check the pickles daily to make sure no mold is forming. If you do see mold, you'll have to throw away your pickles and start over.

8. If the brine level begins to fall below the top of the pickles, top it off with more salt water.

9. Start tasting after 4 days. When the pickles are to your liking, refrigerate them, which will slow the fermentation. The pickles will continue to ferment, but if kept under refrigeration, they will not spoil.

HOW DID THAT HAPPEN? *When you ferment cucumbers to make pickles, you put them in a solution of salt and water called brine. Brine is about 7 percent salt. That's twice as salty as ocean water. Only two kinds of bacteria (both of which are good) can thrive at that level of salinity,* Leuconostoc mesenteroides *and* Lactobacillus plantarum.

All bacteria, both helpful and harmful, produce acids as they grow. As your cucumbers sit in their saltwater bath, those acids make the brine sour. At a certain point, the brine gets so sour that the Leuconostoc *bacteria can't survive and the* Lactobacillus *take over.* Lactobacillus *are the same bacteria that turn milk into yogurt. They're also the main beneficial bacteria used in making fermented foods like cheese, pickles, sauerkraut, Korean kimchi, Japanese miso, and Indian lassi. If you've ever heard people talk about the healthfulness of probiotic foods, they're talking about the benefits of eating a diet high in* Lactobacillus *bacteria.*

FRUIT TO BOOT LEATHER

How can something as soft and moist and fragile as fruit become something as tough and pliable as leather? It's easy. All it takes is a blender, an oven, and a lot of time. Fruit is filled with lots of solid fiber. When the fruit is fresh and ripe, that fiber is dispersed in a sea of water and air. And when you bite into that fruit, it gushes juice (that's the water coming out) and it collapses (that's the air being released). To turn fresh fruit into fruit leather, you get rid of the water and air, yielding a thin sheet of chewy (and naturally sweet) fruit fiber.

Makes about ½ pound (230 g)

 BE CAREFUL! HAVE A GROWN-UP HELP YOU DO THIS.

GET THIS:

1¼ pounds (570 g) ripe fruit of your choice, such as:
    10 medium plums, skin-on, pitted and chopped
    4 medium peaches or nectarines, skin-on, pitted and chopped
    3 large apples, skin-on, chopped
    1 quart (1 L) strawberries, hulled and chopped
    2 medium peeled bananas, chopped
    5 cups (570 g) raspberries or blueberries
¾ cup (150 g) sugar
1 tablespoon (15 ml) lemon juice

Rimmed cookie sheet
Silicone baking pad or aluminum foil
Blender
Medium saucepan
Mixing spoon
Icing spatula
Wire cooling rack
Sheet of waxed paper
Scissors
Gallon-sized zipper-lock plastic bag

(continued)

COOL

YUM!

EASY-PEASY

AFTERNOON PROJECT

GO SHOP

LESS THAN $10

WATCH OUT!

DO THIS:

GET EVERYTHING READY

1. Preheat the oven to 200°F (95°C).
2. Line the cookie sheet with the silicone baking pad or aluminum foil.

MUSH THE FRUIT

1. Put fruit, sugar, and lemon juice in the blender and blend on high until smooth.

BOIL THE LEATHER

1. Pour the mushed-up fruit into the saucepan and bring to a boil over medium-high heat, stirring most of the time. (GET AN ADULT TO HELP YOU DO THIS!)
2. Reduce the heat to medium-low and cook until the fruit is very thick, stirring a lot, especially near the end.

BAKE THE LEATHER

1. Pour the leather goo into the prepared cookie sheet. Use the spatula to spread into an even, super-thin layer. Try to get the entire bottom of the pan covered.
2. Bake until the top feels only a tiny bit sticky, about 3 hours.

COOL, CUT, AND EAT

1. Let cool completely in the pan on the wire rack. Peel off the mat or foil. If the leather still feels wet on the bottom, you can put it back on the pan, wet-side up, and bake for another 30 minutes to dry out.
2. Put the leather on the sheet of waxed paper. With the scissors, cut through both the fruit leather and the paper to make individual strips.
3. Eat as much as you want, then roll up the leftover strips and store in the zipper-lock bag for up to 1 week.

HOW DID THAT HAPPEN? *Fruit leather is dried-up jam, and jam is just mashed-up fruit cooked with sugar. The added sugar increases the thickness of the fruit mush by loading it up with millions of grains of sugar that absorb the juice, causing it to get thick. That's why jam spreads nicely on your toast, where a smashed strawberry would just be wet and runny.*

Here, when you spread the jam into a thin layer on the cookie sheet, you expose it to a lot of air, which allows the moisture in the mixture to evaporate. When you put it in the oven, the warm air sucks up even more of the moisture. Eventually, the jam has so little moisture in it that it loses its stickiness and becomes a solid that can be picked up without making a mess.

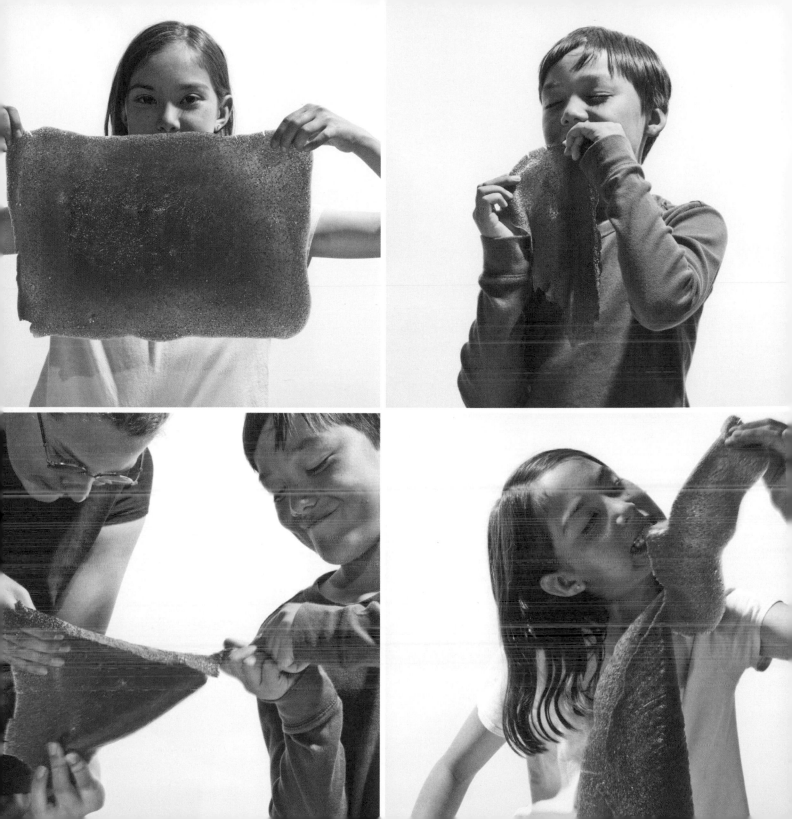

WHAT COLOR IS THE CABBAGE?

Did you know that vegetable colors can change? Depending on how you store or cook a vegetable, you can turn green vegetables brown, purple vegetables red, and red vegetables blue.

Makes 6 servings

 BE CAREFUL! HAVE A GROWN-UP HELP YOU DO THIS.

CRAZY!

EAT UP!

EASY-PEASY

LESS THAN 30 MINUTES

GO SHOP

LESS THAN $5

BE CAREFUL

GET THIS:

2 tablespoons (30 ml) vegetable oil

4 cups (350 g) thinly sliced red cabbage

¼ cup (60 ml) water

1 tart apple, like Granny Smith, peeled, cored, and shredded

¼ cup (60 ml) apple cider vinegar

¼ cup (50 g) sugar

Salt and pepper to taste

Large frying pan

Mixing spoon

DO THIS:

SAUTÉ THE CABBAGE

1. Heat the oil in the frying pan. Add the cabbage. What color is it?
2. Heat, stirring to cook evenly, until it starts to look cooked.
3. Add the water and bring to a boil. What happened to the color?

CHANGE THE COLOR

1. Add the apple, vinegar, and sugar.
2. Bring to a boil. What happens to the color now?
3. Boil until tender, about 3 minutes.
4. Season to taste with salt and pepper, and enjoy.

 HOW DID THAT HAPPEN? *A chemical called anthocyanin is the purple pigment in red cabbage. In the universe of vegetable colors, anthocyanins are the weirdest. They actually change color depending on their environment. Mix them with an acid, like vinegar, and they stay bright red. Water them down, and the color becomes so pale it almost disappears. Expose them to something alkaline (a base), like tap water or baking soda, and they turn turquoise-blue—awesome, and so-o-o-o strange looking.*

POLKA-DOT CELERY

YOWZA!

EAT UP!

EASY-PEASY

TWO PHASES

GATHER AT HOME

LESS THAN $5

SAFE

Celery on its own is pretty pale stuff. But stick it in a glass of food coloring, and it develops the loveliest case of polka dots and stripes. The patterns are made by the food coloring traveling through the natural veins in the celery stem, and the same thing will happen with any stem vegetable—fennel, asparagus, Swiss chard, or rhubarb—or with any colored liquid (although food coloring works best because the color is so saturated). If you try this experiment with a spinach leaf or a fruit vegetable, like a cucumber, the color will be absorbed as a general stain—no pattern at all. That's because those plant parts don't have the same kind of vein structure.

GET THIS:

¼ cup (60 ml) red or blue food coloring

3 or 4 celery stalks, preferably with leaves

8-ounce (240 ml) drinking glass

DO THIS:

SET UP YOUR CELERY

1. Fill the drinking glass with water and add the food coloring.
2. Cut a slice from the wide ends of the celery stalks and put the celery, cut-end down, into the colored water.

SET ASIDE AND WATCH WHAT HAPPENS

1. Watch carefully and you'll see that, after about one day, the food coloring will get sucked up through the stems of the celery stalks. When you slice the celery, the slices will be polka-dotted with red or blue.
2. Set aside for 2 more days. By that time, the food coloring will have traveled all the way up the celery stalks into the leaves, and the leaves will have started to turn red or blue, too.

HOW DID THAT HAPPEN? *All vegetables are parts of plants. Celery stalks are stems. The job of the stem is to transport water and nutrients from the plant's roots into its leaves, fruit, and flowers, and to transport energy generated in the leaves down to the roots for storage. Once the celery is harvested, it's no longer connected to the root of the plant, but given the opportunity to do its job, it still tries. When you stick the celery into the liquid, it will draw that liquid up through its vascular system into its leaves. When the liquid is colored, the color stains the veins. Then, when you cut the stalk in slices, you see the cross-section of those veins as dots.*

NEVER-FEAR ALFREDO

COOL

YUM!

A LITTLE HELP, PLEASE!

30–60 MINUTES

GO SHOP

LESS THAN $10

BE CAREFUL

Have you ever tried fettuccine Alfredo? It's the creamiest, richest, most delicious pasta dish you can get. But it's also full of fat. A single portion from a restaurant can contain more than 100 percent of a day's worth of fat, and more than 200 percent of the amount of saturated fat in a recommended healthy diet.

In this Alfredo, almost all that fat is taken out, but the creamy richness is still there, all because of a secret ingredient: cauliflower, and its magical arsenal of pectin!

Makes 4 servings

 BE CAREFUL! HAVE A GROWN-UP HELP YOU DO THIS.

GET THIS:

1 tablespoon (20 g) salt

12 ounces (340 g) fettuccine

1 cup (240 ml) milk

2 heads of cauliflower, trimmed of leaves, cored, and broken into florets

1 tablespoon (15 g) butter

1 tablespoon (10 g) minced garlic

¼ teaspoon ground black pepper

¼ cup (20 g) freshly grated Parmesan cheese

Big pot

Colander

Big heatproof bowl

Blender

Ladle

DO THIS:

BOIL THE NOODLES

1. Fill the big pot about three-fourths full of water and bring to a boil.
2. Stir in the salt.
3. Add fettuccine and boil until tender, about 10 minutes.

DRAIN THE NOODLES

1. Put the colander in the big heatproof bowl. Pour the noodles and water through the colander, catching most of the water in the bowl.
2. Lift the colander from the bowl and set aside.

BOIL THE CAULIFLOWER

1. Return about 3 cups (720 ml) of the reserved pasta water to the pot (save the rest). Add the milk and cauliflower.
2. Put over medium-high heat and bring to a simmer. Simmer until the cauliflower is tender, about 8 minutes.

MAKE THE SAUCE

1. Transfer everything from the cauliflower pot to the blender and purée. You may need to do this in two batches, depending on the size of your blender.
2. Wipe the pot clean, add the butter, and melt over medium heat.
3. Add the garlic and cook, stirring, until you can smell garlic strongly. Don't let it brown! It will only take about 1 minute.
4. Add the cooked noodles and a ladleful of the pasta water. Stir until the noodles separate from one another.
5. Add the puréed cauliflower and the pepper. Bring to a simmer, stirring to coat all the noodles with sauce. Cook gently until the sauce is creamy and just thick enough to coat the noodles. Add more pasta water if the sauce gets too thick.

EAT

1. Remove from the heat and stir in the cheese.
2. Dish up and dig in!

HOW DID THAT HAPPEN? *Cauliflower is a powerhouse of pectin, the glue of the food world. Made up of long chains of starchy molecules that bond together into a gummy paste, pectin helps hold together the walls of plant cells. When you boil cauliflower, its cell walls soften, releasing their pectin. Then, when you mash the cauliflower, that pectin makes the resulting purée creamy and thick, a lot like a sauce made from butter and cream.*

VEGETABLE-DYED EGGS

Before the days of packaged dyes, all Easter eggs were colored with pigments extracted from vegetables. It's easy and very cool to isolate the green from spinach leaves, the red from cranberries, and the purple from a head of cabbage. And once you've got the pigment out, you can make the most amazing paintings or dyed eggs. When you extract the color from natural objects, like vegetables, flowers, and minerals, you are practicing an ancient art. At one time, much of the training in being a painter included learning to extract pigments from nature and stabilize them into paint. When Leonardo da Vinci (who was as famous a scientist as he was an artist) painted the *Mona Lisa*, he had to start by getting all the vegetables he needed to make his paint.

Makes 12 eggs

 BE CAREFUL! HAVE A GROWN-UP HELP YOU DO THIS.

GET THIS:

About 2 cups produce (170 to 230 g) to make your dyestuff:

Reds: Red onion skin, cranberries, raspberries, beets, pomegranate

Oranges: Carrots, yellow onion skin, orange rind, paprika (use ¼ cup/30 g)

Yellows: Lemon or orange peel, green tea, chamomile tea, ground turmeric (use ¼ cup/30 g)

Greens: Golden apple peel, spinach leaves, liquid chlorophyll (available online)

Blues: Red cabbage leaves, purple grape juice

Purples: Hibiscus tea, small amount of purple grape juice, Red Zinger tea

2 tablespoons (60 ml) white vinegar

12 hard-cooked eggs, in the shell

Vegetable or mineral oil (optional)

Medium saucepan

Fine-mesh sieve

1-quart (1-L) glass measuring cup

Crayons or wax pencils (optional)

Rubber bands (optional)

Slotted spoon

Wire cooling rack

Clean piece of sponge (optional)

(continued)

DO THIS:

MAKE THE DYE

1. Put your dyestuff in the saucepan and cover with water. (Note that purple grape juice and liquid chlorophyll need no cooking—just rub directly on the egg.)
2. Bring to a boil, turn the heat down to low, and simmer for 15 minutes.
3. Check the color by dipping a piece of paper towel into the dye. If it doesn't look colorful enough, simmer the dye for another 15 minutes.
4. Pour the dye through the sieve into the measuring cup. Stir in the vinegar.

DYE THE EGGS

1. Wash the eggs with soapy water to remove any oil from the surface.
2. If you want, you can draw on the eggshells with crayon or something else waxy. The eggshell won't absorb dye on the areas you colored. You can also tie-dye your eggs by wrapping rubber bands of varying thickness around them. Once the eggs are dyed and dried, just remove the rubber bands to reveal the design. (If you want to eat the eggs right away, you can shell them before dyeing—and then feast on a rainbow of hard boiled eggs!)
3. Use the slotted spoon to lower the eggs into the dye. Leave them in the dye until you get the color you want. The longer they stay in the dye, the deeper the color will be.

DRY AND FINISH

1. Remove the eggs with the slotted spoon and put on the wire rack to dry.
2. Naturally dyed eggs have a dull finish. For a textured finish, dab the eggs with a bit of clean sponge before the dye dries. If you want to make them semi-glossy, you can rub them with some vegetable or mineral oil once they're dry.

 HOW DID THAT HAPPEN? *There are four families of plant pigments:*

__Chlorophyll__, found in green leafy vegetables, is green.

__Caratenoids__, found in carrots, peppers, tomatoes, and watermelon, make reds, oranges, and yellows.

__Anthocyanins__, found in cabbage berries, radishes, and potatoes, make reds and purples.

__Betaines__, found in beets, chard, and cactus pear, make reds and yellows.

Although most dyes used to color fabric or jelly beans or Easter eggs are now made from artificial ingredients, at one time all the pigments in paints and dyes came from nature—stones, soil, bugs, and vegetables.

Getting the color out of a vegetable isn't hard: just chop them up and steep out the color, the same way you would make tea. Once your color tea is made, you need to acidify it to get it to stick to the egg. Eggs are largely protein, which are weak acids and are looking to attach themselves to stronger acids. By mixing vinegar into your dye, you create a strong acid that the proteins in the egg eagerly attach themselves to.

DIY MICROWAVE POPCORN

COOL

YUM!

EASY-PEASY

LESS THAN 30 MINUTES

GATHER AT HOME

LESS THAN $5

SAFE

Make your own sure-pop bags and you'll never have to buy a box of microwave popcorn again. That's going to save you money, in addition to teaching you all about exploding vegetables. One pound of regular popping corn is enough to make 50 bags of microwave popcorn. The dried kernels sold as "popping corn" come from a special variety of corn cultivated to explode into large, crunchy-soft pillows. You can find bags of it in the same part of a grocery store that sells the microwavable stuff. Just make sure the corn you buy is fresh (check the date on the bag). Kernels of old popping corn tend to crack with age. Once that happens, pressure can't build up inside the kernel and the corn will fizzle, like a dead firecracker.

Makes 1 single-serving bag

GET THIS:

¼ cup (40 g) regular (bulk) popping corn
  (not prepackaged in individual bags)
½ teaspoon salt (you can also buy popcorn salt,
  which is ground finer than regular salt)
Any other seasoning you want, like
  garlic powder, cinnamon, chili powder, etc.
1 teaspoon (5 ml) olive oil

Measuring cup
Teaspoon
Brown paper lunch bag
Microwave oven

DO THIS:

SET UP

1. Put all the ingredients in the bag and fold the opening of the bag over twice.
2. Shake gently to mix everything together and press on the bag to force out the air.

GET POPPING!

1. Set the bag on its back (unfolded side) in the microwave and cook until the pops dwindle down to one every 10 seconds. For most microwaves, this will take about 4 minutes, but if yours is high-powered, it could take as few as 2 minutes, so listen to what's going on.

DIG IN

1. Open the bag carefully so you don't get hurt by escaping steam.
2. Pour into a bowl and dig in!

HOW DID THAT HAPPEN? *Popcorn is made from a variety of corn with a tough hull that dries while leaving some moisture in the center of the kernel. Once it's heated to 212°F (100°C), steam builds up inside the kernel. When the temperature reaches about 380°F (190°C), the built-up pressure explodes the tough hull and turns the kernel inside out. The steam puffs up the grain's mixture of protein and starch into a light, flaky exterior.*

MILKING NUTS

Sad as it may seem, some people are "lactose intolerant." That means they can't digest the sugars in dairy foods such as milk, cheese, or ice cream, which are usually made from cow's milk. Fortunately, though, there are some great non-dairy alternatives—including milks made from soy, rice, and even nuts! People around the world have enjoyed nut milks for centuries. By soaking and then finely puréeing almonds, cashews, or hazelnuts, for instance, you can make a delicious, non-dairy drink that's packed with calcium, proteins, vitamins, and minerals. You can even use it just like milk. Pour it on your cereal or make it into chocolate milk; use it when you cook or bake, or just enjoy a nice, cold cup of creamy nut milk.

YOWZA!

YUM!

EASY-PEASY

TWO PHASES

GO SHOP

LESS THAN $5

SAFE

Makes about 3 cups (720 ml)

GET THIS:

2½ cups (300 g) raw almonds or cashews

Blender
Fine-mesh sieve or nut-milk bag (available in natural-food stores)
1-quart (1-L) glass container—a measuring cup works great

DO THIS:

SOAK THE NUTS

1. Put the nuts in the blender and add hot water to cover.
2. Set aside for at least an hour, or as long as overnight.

MILK 'EM!

1. Blend the nuts and soaking water until completely smooth.
2. Pour the nut milk through the sieve or nut milk bag. If using a nut milk bag, you'll have to squeeze the bag to get all the milk to come through.

DRINK YOUR MILK

1. Refrigerate until well-chilled, at least an hour.
2. Pour yourself a glass, or pour it over your breakfast cereal, or use it to make Easy Almond Pudding (page 125).
3. Store in a tightly covered container for up to a week.

(continued)

HOW DID THAT HAPPEN? *Milk is a nutritious liquid made by mothers to feed their babies. It's a combination of protein, fat, sugar, and minerals distilled from the mother's diet into a form that's easy for babies to drink. In the wild, animals only drink the milk of their mothers, but throughout history, people have learned to use the milk of other animals, and to derive milk from plants to feed themselves.*

Not every vegetable can yield milk, but some beans, seeds, and nuts—the parts of plants that have high concentrations of proteins and fats—can be processed into creamy, nutritious substitutes for dairy milk. Those proteins and fats provide nutrition for a plant when it's first starting out, growing from a baby seed into a mature plant with roots, stems, and leaves, parts it will use to gather nutrition from the sun and soil. (No wonder nuts and seeds are so good for you!) When you grind up dried nuts into nut butters (like peanut butter and almond butter), the oils in the nuts are pulverized into a paste. But if you soak the nuts in water before grinding them, the oils come out, suspended in the water. When the solid particles of nuts are drained off, you're left with a liquid that is very similar to animal milk.

easy almond pudding

Makes 4 servings

GET THIS:

⅓ cup (65 g) sugar

2 tablespoons (16 g) cornstarch

¼ teaspoon salt

2½ cups (600 ml) almond milk

3 large egg yolks (see page 78 for tips on how to
separate eggs)

3 tablespoons (45 g) unsalted butter, cut in chunks

1 teaspoon (5 ml) vanilla extract

½ teaspoon almond extract

Medium saucepan

Whisk

Small container with a lid for saving egg whites

Wooden mixing spoon

Rubber spatula

4 dessert dishes

Plastic wrap

DO THIS:

MIX IT UP

1. Mix the sugar, cornstarch, and salt together in the saucepan.
2. Whisk in ¼ cup (60 ml) of the almond milk until the mixture is smooth.
3. Whisk in the egg yolks and the remaining 2¼ cups (540 ml) almond milk. (Save the egg whites for another use;
   store in an airtight container in the refrigerator for up to 3 days, or freeze for up to a year.)

COOK IT

1. Cook over medium heat, stirring with the wooden spoon most of the time. Make sure you get the spoon into the
   corners of the pot.
2. When the pudding gets thick and starts to bubble, switch back to the (clean) whisk to get out any lumps.
   BE CAREFUL! THICK LIQUIDS LIKE PUDDING CAN SPIT AND SPUTTER WHEN THEY BOIL.
3. Turn the heat down to low so the pudding bubbles gently (no splattering allowed) and stir with the rubber spatula,
   scraping the bottom of the pan as you stir. Do this for 3 minutes.
4. Remove from the heat and stir in the butter and extracts. Stir until the butter is melted and everything is
   well blended.

CHILL IT

1. Pour the pudding into the 4 dessert dishes, dividing it evenly.
2. Cover each with the plastic wrap, lightly pressing the wrap against the surface of the pudding to keep a skin
   from forming.
3. Refrigerate until chilled, about 2 hours—and enjoy!

CHAPTER 5

EGGCELLENT EGGSPERIMENTS

Eggs have been described as the perfect food. That's because they have a great nutritional balance of protein, fat, and carbs. But they're not just good for eating! Eggs can teach you about how proteins and fats behave, and make you smart about minerals, air pressure, emulsification, filtering, and gels.

All of these experiments are delicious, except for one: Glowy, Bouncy Eggs (page 129) aren't quite as edible as everything else. They're just radical fun.

IN THIS CHAPTER:

GLOWY, BOUNCY EGGS

CHOCOLATE BLAST

MAYO SHAKE

CLEARING UP A SOUPY SITUATION

SOLID SOUP

GLOWY, BOUNCY EGGS

Have you ever tried to bounce an egg? Well, don't try it—at least, not until you try this project. In this experiment, you're going to soak a raw egg in vinegar until the shell dissolves. Eggs are amazing. Right under the shell, there are two membranes. These membranes are made largely of protein, and that protein is going to react with the vinegar in your setup and become firm and bouncy—strong enough to hold all of the liquid egg inside once the shell is gone. The clear liquid (egg white) inside is also packed with proteins. When you shine a light through it, the proteins refract the light and the egg white starts to glow. If you look even more closely, you'll see two lines in the egg white going from the edge to the center. These are "chalazae" (say "cha-LAY-zee"), which are twisted ropes of protein that attach the yolk to the outside membranes and make sure it stays safely in the center of the egg.

WOW!

YUK!

EASY-PEASY

TWO PHASES

GATHER AT HOME

LESS THAN $5

SAFE

Makes 1 glowy, bouncy egg—but make as many as you like!

GET THIS:

1 egg
1½ cups (360 ml) white vinegar

1-quart (1-L) glass jar with lid, like a Mason jar
Soupspoon, if needed

DO THIS:

SET UP YOUR EXPERIMENT

1. Carefully place the egg in the jar. Don't let the egg drop in and break! (If your fingers don't reach the bottom of the jar, ask an adult to help, or put the egg onto a soupspoon, turn the jar sideways on a table or counter, and carefully use the spoon to slide the egg into the jar.)
2. Add the vinegar, screw the lid on tightly, and set the jar aside for 2 to 3 days.

CHECK YOUR EGG!

1. Your egg is ready when you can see these things happening: The vinegar looks foamy, with little bits of decomposed egg shell floating on the surface; the egg has swelled to about twice its size and is floating in the vinegar; you can see light coming through the egg when you hold it up to a window or lightbulb. When you see this happening, it means most of the shell has dissolved. If there are a few opaque areas where light is not coming through, that doesn't matter. They can be washed off.

(continued)

2. Carefully remove the egg from the vinegar and wash in a bowl of cold, clean water. Bounce it, but not too hard. The membrane around the egg has toughened up, but the egg inside is still raw. If the membrane breaks, the raw egg will run all over.

 HOW DID THAT HAPPEN? *The acetic acid in vinegar dissolves the calcium carbonate of the egg shell, causing the shell to dissolve. As soon as you put the egg in the vinegar, you can see bubbles rising off the egg shell. The bubbles are carbon dioxide, created by the reaction of the vinegar and calcium in the egg shell. At the same time, the acid coagulates the protein in the membrane under the shell, making it tough and bouncy.*

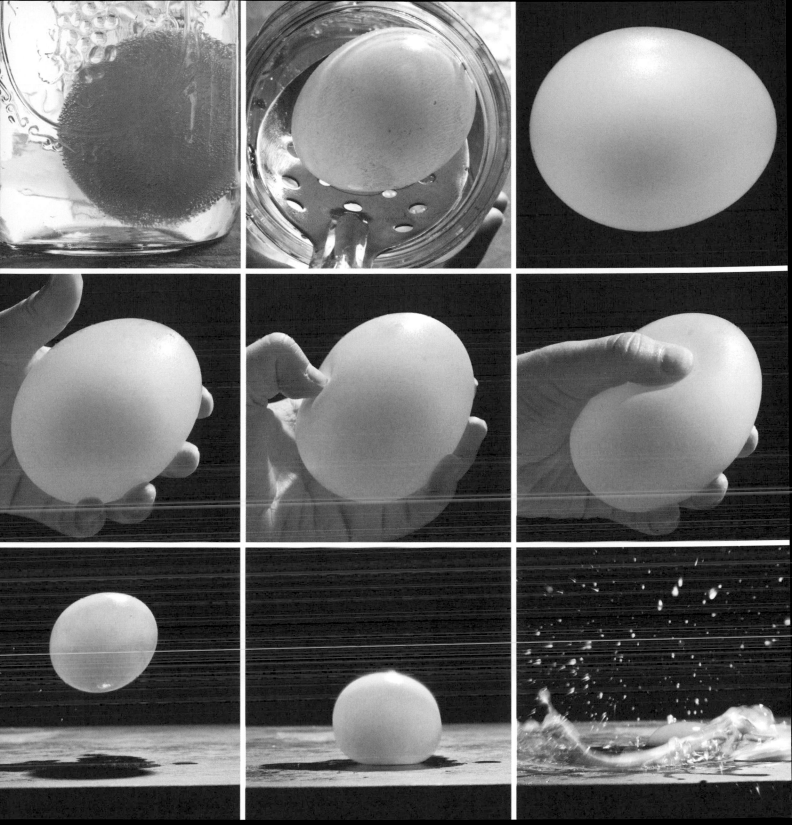

CHOCOLATE BLAST

YOWZA!

YUM!

EASY-PEASY

LESS THAN 30 MINUTES

GATHER AT HOME

LESS THAN $5

SAFE

In this easy experiment, a simple (and delicious) chocolate mixture is forced to rise up and out of its glass container. Eventually it falls back down, just in time for you to eat it for dessert. The intense chocolatiness of each spoonful comes from one ingredient—cocoa powder. Cocoa is concentrated chocolate. All of the fat and fiber that are parts of a cacao bean (the vegetable that we get chocolate from) have been removed, leaving behind the intense, unadulterated taste of chocolate. You don't need a lot of cocoa to get a lot of chocolate flavor, and it's pretty low in calories (if you're counting)—that is, until you add sugar and fat to make it taste sweet and rich.

Makes 1 serving

GET THIS:

3 tablespoons (45 g) sugar

2 tablespoons (10 g) unsweetened
   cocoa powder

1 tablespoon (8 g) all-purpose flour

3 tablespoons (45 ml) milk

1 tablespoon (15 ml) Canola or other bland oil

¼ teaspoon vanilla extract

1 egg

Tall drinking glass

Fork

Small bowl

Small whisk or egg beater

Microwave oven

Spoon

DO THIS:

MAKE THE BATTER

1. Put everything but the egg in the drinking glass.
2. Mix with the fork to combine thoroughly. Make sure you get all of the flour and sugar on the bottom of the glass mixed in.
3. Put the egg in the bowl, beat with the whisk until foamy, and stir into the batter in the glass.

BLAST OFF!

1. Put the glass in the microwave and cook on high for 70 seconds.
2. Watch the batter grow and blast out of the glass.
3. Remove from the microwave. Wait a minute for the mixture to cool; it will deflate.
4. Eat up with the spoon.

(continued)

HOW DID THAT HAPPEN? *The chocolate mixture you made is similar to a French dish called a soufflé (say "soo-FLAY"), a casserole lightened with beaten egg that rises high out of its baking dish and looks amazing.*

When air is heated, it spreads out. If that air is contained in some sort of membrane, like the protein in an egg, it makes the air inside the membrane lighter than the air outside, so the contained air starts to rise. It's the same kind of thing that makes hot-air balloons rise: A balloon is filled with air, a flame heats up the air, the air expands, and the balloon rises. Hotter air equals higher flight. The same thing happens to the air inside your batter. As it heats in the microwave, the batter rises up and out of the glass. When it cools, it deflates, but fortunately it still tastes just as delicious.

MAYO SHAKE

Mayonnaise, a classic French sauce made from eggs and oil, used to be very fancy stuff that only chefs made. Today, everyone buys it in a jar. But if you've got a few minutes and a hand-held immersion blender, making mayo is a snap. And it teaches you about emulsions—the magical technique for making two things, like oil and water, that don't want to come together, come together. Note that this experiment contains raw egg yolk. Raw egg can contain salmonella bacteria, although the risk isn't great. Ask about where your eggs came from. If they came from a reliable farm or have been irradiated, the threat of salmonella has been taken care of.

YOWZA!

YUM!

EASY-PEASY

LESS THAN 30 MINUTES

GATHER AT HOME

LESS THAN $5

SAFE

Makes about 1½ cups (360 ml)

GET THIS:

1 egg
1 teaspoon (5 ml) brown mustard
Juice of ½ lemon
Big pinch of salt
1 cup (240 ml) Canola or other bland oil

1-pint (500-ml) Mason jar
Immersion blender

DO THIS:

1. Put everything in the jar.
2. Insert the blender, turn on high, and blend until thick and creamy, about 1 minute. *Voilà*: Mayonnaise.

HOW DID THAT HAPPEN? *Mayonnaise is an emulsion of oil and water—two liquids that generally don't get along. In mayo, though, they're held together by emulsifiers, mostly lecithin, a protein found in egg yolk.*

Emulsifiers have a unique two-headed chemical structure: One head is attracted to fats, while the other is attracted to water. By burying their fat-loving heads in the oil, their water-loving heads are exposed, allowing them to attach to the water in the egg and lemon juice. The result: Both the fat and the water coexist peacefully in a perfectly creamy sauce.

CLEARING UP A SOUPY SITUATION

CRAZY!

YUM!

A LITTLE HELP, PLEASE!

LESS THAN 30 MINUTES

GATHER AT HOME

LESS THAN $5

SOME COOKING

There's nothing more welcome on a cold day than a rich, steaming bowl of beautiful, clear broth. But is it really clear? Look closely, and you'll probably be able to see teeny, tiny pieces of the meats and vegetables that went into making that soup. In this experiment, you're going to create a food filter that will take out all those micro pieces and leave you with something you've probably never seen—crystal clear soup. You might suspect that you are filtering out some flavor and nutrition along with these microscopic bits, but that can't happen. While the flavorful and nutritious ingredients in the soup are breaking down during cooking, they are giving up everything they have to the broth. By the time a soup is done cooking, all of the bits of carrot and chicken floating in the liquid are just shells of their former selves; the broth has got it all.

Makes 12 servings

 BE CAREFUL! HAVE A GROWN-UP HELP YOU DO THIS.

GET THIS:

8 ounces (230 g) boneless, skinless chicken breast, chopped

2 egg whites, lightly beaten (see page 78 for tips on how to separate eggs)

3 cups (720 ml) chicken broth (not bouillon), either homemade or store-bought

Blender

Medium saucepan

Fine-mesh sieve or clean gold coffee filter

Heatproof glass bowl

Ladle

DO THIS:

MIX IT UP

1. Put all the ingredients in the blender and blend until you have smooth mush.
2. Pour the mixture into the saucepan.

CLEAR IT UP

1. Put the pan over medium-high heat and cook, stirring and scraping the bottom of the pan to make sure the egg white isn't sticking to the bottom.
2. As the solidifying ingredients rise, they act as a filter, straining out all of the murky stuff in the broth. When they reach the top, they'll look like a thick, dirty foam, or "raft." Don't touch the foam, or you'll send the mucky stuff back into the soup.
3. Simmer at medium-low for 5 to 10 minutes.

STRAIN IT

1. Put the fine-mesh sieve over the heatproof bowl.
2. Using the ladle, lift off a small area of the foam on one side of the surface of the soup in the pan and throw it away. Try to get as little soup in the ladle as possible. Wash off the ladle.
3. Stick your ladle back through the hole you made and carefully ladle out the soup from under the foam raft (without disturbing the foam) into the sieve, so the clear soup flows into the bowl.

ISN'T CLEAR BEAUTIFUL?

1. Look at the crystal-clear, beautiful soup you made. Now take a taste; it should be rich and chickeny.

HOW DID THAT HAPPEN? *Soup broth is filled with microscopic bits of oil and food particles that scatter light and keep it from shining through without interruption. In other words, they keep the broth from being clear.*

When you disperse egg white in a soup, you add even more micro particles, making the broth look even cloudier than before. But egg white is a liquid when cold, and gradually solidifies as it heats. As the soup warms up, the dispersed egg white solidifies into a web, trapping all of the microscopic particles in the broth into its tightening net. At a certain point, the web becomes so solid that it separates from the soup and floats to the top, taking all of the captured bits with it. The raft of trapped debris floating on the surface of the soup looks dirty and gross, but the soup underneath is now crystal clear and delicious.

SOLID SOUP

Liquids can be watery and liquids can be thick. But can liquids be solid? Gels are solid liquids, but their solidity is completely dependent on temperature. Gelatin is solid at room temperature, but slip a spoonful into your mouth and, *Presto! Chango!*, your body heat turns it back into liquid again.

Custards are gels in which egg is the solidifying agent. Egg-thickened gels behave differently than gelatins. Once custard sets, it can't become fluid again without breaking apart. But egg adds much more than gelling agent; it brings flavor and rich texture and lots of nutrition to the gel. In this experiment, mixing egg into soup changes its whole state of being!

Makes 1 serving

 BE CAREFUL! HAVE A GROWN-UP HELP YOU DO THIS.

YOWZA!

YUM!

A LITTLE HELP, PLEASE!

LESS THAN 30 MINUTES

GATHER AT HOME

LESS THAN $5

SOME COOKING

GET THIS:

2 eggs, lightly beaten

1½ cups (360 ml) chicken broth

1 teaspoon (5 ml) balsamic vinegar

1 scallion, thinly sliced (optional)

1 teaspoon (5 ml) soy sauce

¼ teaspoon sesame oil

1-quart (1-L) glass measuring cup

Whisk or mixing spoon

Soup bowl that will fit inside the saucepan (below)

Steaming basket or steaming rack

Large, deep saucepan

Plate that fits on top of the soup bowl, or a sheet of aluminum foil

DO THIS:

MIX EVERYTHING UP

1. Mix the eggs and broth in the measuring cup until everything is well blended, and then pour it into the soup bowl. (If you want, you can mix it in a blender and then pour it in the bowl.)
2. Stir in the vinegar.

STEAM IT

1. Put the steamer basket or rack in the saucepan. Add about 1 inch (2.5 cm) of water, but make sure it doesn't touch the bottom of the steamer. Bring to a simmer over medium heat.
2. Put the soup bowl in the basket or on the rack. Cover the bowl with the plate or foil.
3. Cover the pan so that the steam is trapped around the soup bowl and not going out into the air.
4. Reduce the heat to low and simmer until the "soup" is jiggly but solid, about 15 minutes.

(continued)

ENJOY!

1. Uncover, carefully allowing any extra steam to escape. DON'T GET IN THE WAY OF THE ESCAPING STEAM! It can burn you.
2. Scatter the scallion on top and drizzle with soy sauce and sesame oil.
3. Eat with a spoon. Have you ever had solid soup before?

HOW DID THAT HAPPEN? *If you've ever had baked custard, you've eaten sweetened milk solidified by egg. This soup is the same thing, but instead of starting with milk and sugar, we're starting with chicken soup.*

When you heat up egg in almost any liquid, the mixture will solidify. The only liquid that egg will not thicken is plain water. That's because without minerals in the liquid, the negatively charged protein molecules repel one another. But with the positively charged mineral ions clustering around the negatively charged protein, everything relaxes and the liquid sets up.

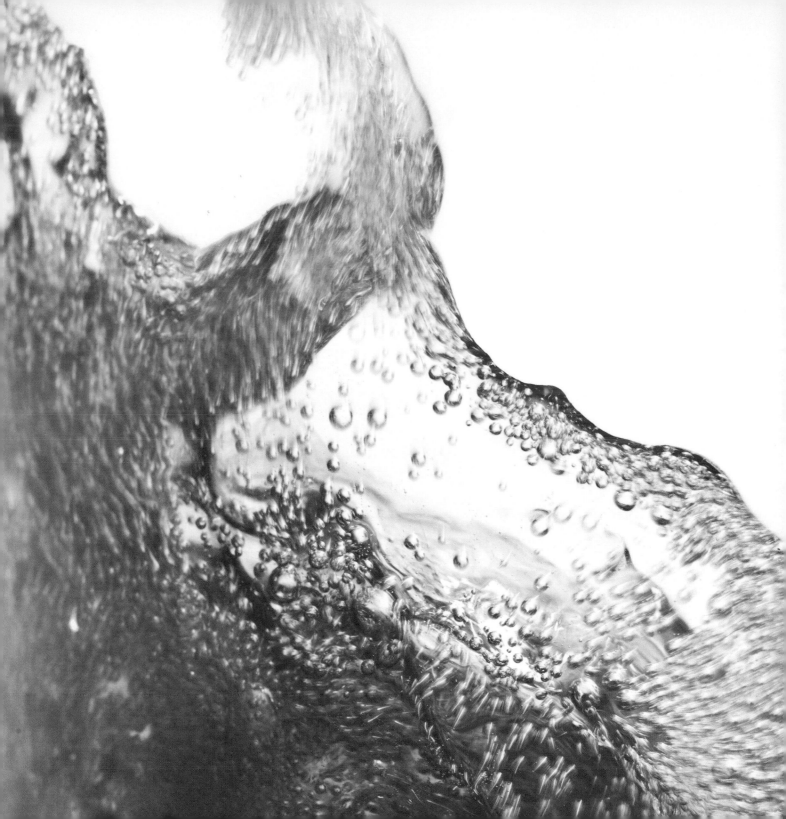

CHAPTER 6

SODALICIOUS EXPERIMENTS

In these experiments, you get to play with the liquids you drink. The first activity takes you through a mind-blowing process of forming an edible bottle around a plop of water. Two other experiments center on fizziness (carbonation), one of the coolest things you can do to a liquid. The last entry takes liquid milk and turns it into a solid.

IN THIS CHAPTER:

LITTLE EDIBLE WATER BOTTLES

COLA CREATIONS: QUICK COLA,

BREWED COLA

natural cola syrup

ROOT BEER GUSHER FLOAT

MILK ROCKS

LITTLE EDIBLE WATER BOTTLES

Making these bite-size water bottles might be one of the freakiest things you ever do. It looks like you're pouring water into more water, and then, before your eyes, the water is enclosed in its own pick-uppable skin. Pop it in your mouth and SPLASH!—instant thirst quencher.

The trick to this experiment is a unique reaction that happens between calcium and a protein in seaweed. All proteins coagulate (firm up). Most do it when exposed to heat. Others do it when mixed with acid, or when agitated with a whisk. Sodium alginate, an extract from brown seaweed, happens to do it when exposed to calcium. Because the reaction is unusual, it looks pretty magical, but it's just chemistry. Sodium alginate has no discernable flavor, so the water in your water bottle just tastes like water.

WOW!

EAT UP!

PLAN IN ADVANCE

30–60 MINUTES

ORDER IN ADVANCE

LESS THAN $5

SAFE

GET THIS:

5½ cups (1.3 l) water

½ teaspoon (2 g) sodium alginate (see recipe introduction; easily available online)

2 teaspoons (8 g) calcium lactate (easily available online)

Small bowl
Measuring cup
Immersion blender
2 large bowls
Tablespoon measuring spoon
Slotted spoon

DO THIS:

MAKE THE SODIUM-ALGINATE MIXTURE

1. In the small bowl, combine 1½ cups (360 ml) of the water and the sodium alginate. Insert the blender and blend until completely dissolved. When fully blended, the mixture will appear cloudy. That's because it's filled with air bubbles.
2. Set aside for 15 minutes to allow the air bubbles to dissipate. When they have, the mixture will be clear.

MAKE THE CALCIUM-LACTATE MIXTURE

1. In one of the large bowls, mix the calcium lactate into the remaining 4 cups (960 ml) water until completely dissolved.

MAKE WATER BOTTLES

1. Gently lower a tablespoon of the sodium-alginate mixture into the calcium-lactate bath
2. The water in the spoon will start to firm around the edges. When that happens, turn the spoon over, encouraging the mixture to slip out as you do. At first, it will look like there isn't anything in the calcium-lactate water, but in a few seconds you'll see a ghostly blob start to form. Let it set for about 3 minutes.

(continued)

3. Fill the second large bowl with clean, cold water. Remove the blob with the slotted spoon or with your fingers and transfer to the clean-water bath to stop the reaction.

4. You can do two at a time once you get some practice.

ENJOY!

1. Lift the "water bottles" from the clean-water bath with a slotted spoon or your fingers. Pop into your mouth and feel the refreshment! Store at room temperature for up to 30 minutes.

HOW DID THAT HAPPEN? *Sodium alginate is an extract of seaweed. It forms a gel in the presence of calcium. Calcium lactate is a powdered calcium. When you dropped one mixture into the other, the surface of the sodium-alginate water gelled as soon as it hit the calcium-lactate water, forming a shell around the water blob. Once the gel formed, the rest of the sodium-alginate mixture stayed as a pool of drinkable water inside its gel casing, creating an edible water bottle.*

COLA CREATIONS: QUICK COLA, BREWED COLA

Soda is just flavored carbonated water. In this experiment, you make a cola syrup and carbonate it two ways: one by mixing the syrup with bottled carbonated water, and the other in a much older way: by brewing it with yeast. Try it both ways and taste the difference.

CRAZY!

YUM!

PLAN IN ADVANCE

TWO PHASES

GO SHOP

LESS THAN $10

SOME COOKING

QUICK COLA

When you have your own stash of cola syrup, you can make your own homemade soda whenever you want.

Makes 1 serving

GET THIS:

½ cup (120 ml) Natural Cola Syrup (page 151)
1½ cups (360 ml) seltzer

Stirring spoon
Tall drinking glass

DO THIS:

JUST STIR AND SERVE!

1. Stir syrup and seltzer in a tall drinking glass to combine.
2. Fill glass with ice, and serve.

(continued)

BREWED COLA

No seltzer needed in this version: add a little yeast, and they'll make the bubbles for you.

Makes 5 qt (5 L)

 BE CAREFUL! HAVE A GROWN-UP HELP YOU DO THIS.

GET THIS:

1 quart (1 L) Natural Cola Syrup (page 151)

4 quarts (4 L) lukewarm (80° to 90°F/27° to 32°C) water

⅛ teaspoon champagne yeast (*Saccharomyces bayanus*), available from homebrew stores or online

Large bowl or pot

Kitchen funnel, cleaned and sanitized

Plastic soda bottles with lids, cleaned and sanitized

DO THIS:

MAKE THE SYRUP MIXTURE

1. Combine the cola syrup and water in the large container.
2. Test the temperature. It should now be about 75° to 80°F (24° to 27°C). Stir in the yeast until completely dissolved.

FILL THE BOTTLES

1. Fill the cleaned, sanitized bottles using a clean, sanitized kitchen funnel.
2. Leave 1¼ inch (3.2 cm) air space in the neck of each bottle.

SEAL AND STORE

1. Seal the bottles and store them at room temperature for 2 to 4 days.
2. When the soda bottles feel rock hard, the soda is fully carbonated. Refrigerate for at least 1 week before serving, but plan to use within 3 weeks. The flavor of the soda improves with time in the refrigerator, but will become overly foamy if held for too long.

HOW DID THAT HAPPEN? *Do you like bubbles in your beverages? Most people do. Naturally carbonated water from underground mineral springs has long been considered healthful, leading to a belief that carbonated beverages in general are good for you. Since the takeover of highly sweetened sodas, though, that belief has been turned upside down. Even so, carbonation has some anti-bacterial properties, and the effect of carbonation enhances the experience of coldness in the mouth. But most of all, the fizz just feels good.*

Aside from using naturally carbonated spring water, the only other ways to get bubbles into your drink is to force them in under pressure (that's the way commercial sodas are carbonated today), or you can add a little bit of yeast and let it do the work for you. That's the way carbonated sodas were manufactured originally. It's not unlike the way beer is brewed. Yeasts use sugar for energy and produce alcohol and carbon-dioxide gas in the process. When making beer, the carbon dioxide is removed and the alcohol remains. When making soda, the carbon dioxide is trapped in the liquid and fermentation is stopped before too much alcohol accumulates.

natural cola syrup

Makes 1 quart (1 L) syrup, enough for 1 gallon (4 L) cola

GET THIS:

Finely grated zest and juice of 2 oranges

Finely grated zest and juice of 1 lemon

Finely grated zest and juice of 1 lime

3 large sticks cinnamon, broken into small pieces

2 teaspoons (10 ml) coriander seed

¼ teaspoon finely grated nutmeg

2 tablespoons (30 ml) dried bitter orange peel

1 quart (1 L) water

4½ cups (900 g) sugar

½ teaspoon vanilla extract

¼ cup (60 ml) caramel color (like Kitchen Bouquet)

Large saucepan

Wooden mixing spoon

1-quart (1-L) jar with a lid, like a Mason jar, or other
   airtight container

DO THIS:

1. In a large saucepan, mix the orange, lemon, and lime zests, the cinnamon pieces, coriander seed, grated nutmeg, bitter orange peel, and water.
2. Stir in the sugar and bring to a boil, stirring until the sugar dissolves. Boil for 1 full minute.
3. Remove from the heat and stir in the citrus juices, vanilla, and caramel color.
4. Cool and strain. Store refrigerated in a tightly covered container for up to 2 weeks.

ROOT BEER GUSHER FLOAT

You may have seen videos showing high-flying soda geysers. This version is not quite as spectacular, but it is way more delicious (you get to drink the soda), and it's controlled enough to do indoors. The taller and narrower your glass, the bigger the gush you'll achieve.

Makes 1 serving

GET THIS:

1 scoop vanilla ice cream

1 cup (240 ml) root beer, chilled

1 to 3 fruit-flavored Mentos mints

Newspaper, plastic cloth, large tray, or
something else to protect the table

Tall drinking glass

Ice cream scoop

Drinking straw

DO THIS:

SET UP

1. Spread out the newspaper or plastic tablecloth on a table. Put the drinking glass on top.
2. Put the scoop of ice cream and the straw in the glass.

LAUNCH AND DRINK UP

1. Add the root beer. It will foam up.
2. Drop in the Mentos and start drinking before the bubbles overflow!

HOW DID THAT HAPPEN? *Sealed in a bottle, the carbon-dioxide gas in your root beer is dispersed and pretty stable. But as soon as the bottle is opened, air from the outside enters—along with a gazillion tiny particles of dust. The suspended gas latches onto these particles and separates from the water. Each molecule forms a little bubble as it hitches a ride up and out. When you add the Mentos, things really take off. The surface of the mint may look smooth, but it's actually covered with millions of tiny dimples that are potential bubble sites. That tiny little mint has enough bubble-making potential to send the bubbles over the top.*

MILK ROCKS

This is the formula for a liquid that makes something you eat, rather than drink. And when you take a bite, you might just recognize what you've made: it's ricotta cheese! That's right, you're about to make cheese—and that's pretty cool. Plus, after you're done making your cheese and straining it, there's going to be a lot of liquid left over, called whey. You can chill the whey and drink it as is, or flavor it with chocolate syrup, puréed fruit, or a little bit of vanilla for an extra treat.

Makes about 10 ounces (285 g) cheese and about 1 quart (1 L) whey

 BE CAREFUL! HAVE A GROWN-UP HELP YOU DO THIS.

CRAZY!

EAT UP!

A LITTLE HELP, PLEASE!

30-60 MINUTES

GATHER AT HOME

LESS THAN $5

SOME COOKING

GET THIS:

½ gallon (2 L) whole milk

¼ cup (60 ml) lemon juice

½ teaspoon salt

Large saucepan

Wooden mixing spoon

Strainer

2 bowls

Cheesecloth or a nut-milk bag, available online or at natural-food stores

Slotted spoon

DO THIS:

HEAT THE MILK

1. Put the milk in the saucepan and cook over medium heat until it's steamy and foamy, stirring all the time. Don't let the milk boil!

ADD THE LEMON JUICE

1. Remove the milk from the heat and stir in the lemon juice.
2. The milk should curdle, separating into little lumps (curds) and a thin liquid (whey).
3. Let the milk sit for about 10 minutes without touching it. At the end of that time, the curds and whey should be completely separated.

STRAIN

1. Set the strainer over one of the bowls and line with cheesecloth or a nut-milk bag.
2. Using the slotted spoon, spoon the curds into the strainer, letting the whey collect in the bowl.
3. Gather up the ends of the cheesecloth and squeeze gently to remove more whey.

(continued)

FINISH THE CHEESE

1. Open the cheesecloth and dump the curd into the other bowl.
2. Gently stir in the salt.
3. Taste your cheese. It should taste like lemony fresh ricotta cheese. Enjoy the cheese and drink the whey, or use the whey for cooking. It's a good milk substitute in baking.

HOW DID THAT HAPPEN? *Milk is a mixture of protein, fat, and milk sugar (called lactose), suspended in water, plus a few minerals. When you add an acid like lemon juice to warm milk, it causes molecules of casein (one of the proteins in milk) to bond to one another. That forms a solid curd, or lump, of protein, fat, fat-soluble vitamins, and minerals. The curd floats in liquid whey (say "way"), a mixture of lactose, non-casein proteins, and water-soluble vitamins and minerals. Although much of the protein and fat in the milk have been collected in the curd, the whey is still sweet and very nutritious. Save it for drinking or cooking. You can use it instead of milk for making pancakes or for baking.*

Acknowledgments

I write food books for my livelihood. Some of the ideas for these books stem from a current interest, a chance conversation, or something that I ate or read. Some of the ideas come from publishers or editors who want to produce a book on a particular subject and who are looking for a writer.

When readers or interviewers ask me where the idea for a book came from, I can feel their disappointment when I tell them that it did not originate with me; as if somehow it is no longer MY book. Well, the fact is, I have never written a book that is exclusively mine. No one ever has. There are always others who inspire and influence and create, and whose work joins with the author's to produce the book that you hold in your hands.

These are the people who built this book:

Leslie Jonath, who figured out the concept for *Amazing (Mostly) Edible Science* and assembled the team, including me, to make it happen.

Ruth Brown, who edited the manuscript and turned it into a book, and just by being herself, added clarity, humor, practical know-how, and smarts to what you're reading.

Chris Rochelle, who got so into taking the ridiculous photos on these pages that he practically had to be tied down to stop shooting at the end of each day. His skill and expertise are what allow you to see an egg explode—so awesome!

Amy Wisniewski, who technically is the food stylist for this book, but that title doesn't begin to describe the attention, intelligence, and kitchen prowess she brought to its contents.

Allison Stern, who designed the pages and the cover and the whole package, so that you can experience something more lively and interactive than my static words and Chris's wacky photos.

Mary Ann Hall and Heather Godin, the publishing force at Quarry, who bought our project and brought it to market, giving us all a chance to make a living doing what we love to do.

All of the kids who experimented with our experiments and made these pages jump with life and the fun of discovery: Vittoria Adams, Eddie Andrews, Anikka Erickson, Hans Erickson, Sarah Jonath, Miel Lappin, and Charlotte Thornton.